Penguin Non-Fiction
This England

20p

MICHAEL BATEMAN, aged thirty-seven, is the typical 'This England' product. He was brought up in Sussex by an uncle who was a retired Indian Army colonel, and educated at public school and Oxbridge. He was commissioned during National Service. All this good work, however, was undone by a three-year spell working on newspapers in the North-east. He was a reporter on the *Daily Herald* and on the *Daily Mail*, is now Atticus on the *Sunday Times*. A contributor to *Punch*, he is also the author of several books of interviews. Michael Bateman, who lives in Putney, is married to Jane Deverson, also a writer, and they have two sons, Daniel and Paul.

This England

Selections from the *New Statesman*
column 1934–1968

Edited by Michael Bateman

Penguin Books

Could you, please, assist me? I am
trying to find a book I read some years ago.
It was a small paper-backed one written
by a lady. In it were given exercises
for mental control, one of which was to
imagine oneself inside a matchbox.

Letter in PREDICTION

Penguin Books Ltd, Harmondsworth, Middlesex, England
Penguin Books Inc., 7110 Ambassador Road, Baltimore, Maryland 21207, U.S.A.
Penguin Books Australia Ltd, Ringwood, Victoria, Australia

This collection first published 1969
Copyright © The Statesman & Nation Publishing Co. Ltd., 1969
Preface copyright © Michael Bateman, 1969

Made and printed in Great Britain by Cox & Wyman Ltd, London, Reading and Fakenham
Set in Monotype Times

Contents

Preface

If you ever wonder where foreigners get such funny ideas about England, the answer is that they get them from the English. This book provides the proof. This comprehensive selection of English attitudes is compiled from some 1,700 issues of the *New Statesman*, where they have appeared as cuttings contributed to the 'This England' column over the life-span of the feature, thirty-five years. As a record of the Englishman's eccentric approach to his monarchy, his Church, his judiciary, his morals and his animals, it's a fascinating document, in which we discover a country where foxes would vote for the continuance of fox-hunting, if, like women, they had the vote; where a reversal in a cricket match is a tragedy 'worse than anything devised by Aeschylus or Euripides', and where High Churchmen explain that their high moral character was developed only by the 'sensible correction' of flogging at school.

Just what is an Englishman?

England, the evidence clearly indicates, is a country 'whose frontiers are defined by God' and an Englishman is the kind of man God chooses 'when He wants something difficult done'. You can recognize an Englishman instantly 'by the cut of his flannels' or by the fact that he's the one 'whose actions are motivated by moral motives entirely regardless of self-interest'. Typically he is 'a jolly good sort, one of those very hearty men ... who wears plus-fours, smokes a pipe and talks about nothing but beer and rugby football'. (Though the wife of this particular man told a court, 'My nerves won't stand much more of it.')

The Englishman accepts his aristocracy as part of the nature of things and is pleased when they show signs of eccentricity. He admires people like the Duke of Norfolk (who shows 'surprising humour' flicking butter-pats at a screen), the Duke of Marlborough (who tosses raspberries to the ceiling and catches them in his mouth as they fall) and the Duke of Gloucester (who is known as Clapper because he claps his hands for his servants). He is not unduly surprised that Sir Paul Dukes walks across a lawn on his hands (to keep fit for the Intelligence Service) or that Duncan Sandys is given an Indian servant by his father for his twenty-first birthday, or that Lady Linlithgow prepares for her vice-regal duty in India by spending one hundred hours before West End fitting room mirrors to 'evolve a magnificent wardrobe'.

The Englishman notes with interest that the Queen Mother listened to the Dales to find out what the middle classes were thinking, and sees nothing amiss in the fact that Burmese and RAF units in Mandalay search three days for a teddy bear lost by Princess Alexandra – twenty-five years old at the time. It seems entirely proper to him that Sir Alec Douglas Home's Nanny should see that at the age of one he 'didn't talk to the servants'.

Where foreigners ask for mere ability from their rulers, the Englishman expects more individual qualities. He admires the oratory of Sir Winston Churchill ('impressive unintelligibility'), or better still the total silence of the Scottish peer, the Earl of Morton, sedulously maintained at the House of Lords until he died at the age of ninety-one. He likes firmness in a politician, as when Quintin Hogg stands his ground and declares that 'the Conservatives do not believe it necessary, and even if it were, we would oppose it', and he respects the man who can occasionally introduce a spiritual note into the banalities of political life and say, like Enoch Powell, 'I am glad there are rich people

about. It affects me like looking at sunsets and snow-capped mountains.'

Rugby and cricket shape the Englishman's character. The original rules of one cricket club forbade players to 'rub' when struck on the shin. A rugby player could boast: 'I was crocked for life in a sportsman's game and I'm proud of it.' A writer could report a rugby match in the *Guardian* as follows: 'Meads was kicked on the head and had to have three stitches put in the cut. Kirkpatrick broke his nose early in the match. Villepreux played most of the game with two ribs broken. Many others were hurt. Some of the injuries were deliberately inflicted. These deeds made unpleasant watching. But, taken as a whole, this was not a game that got out of hand.'

Your Englishman is a Christian, but a thoughtful one, troubled by dilemmas. For example, how to reconcile Christian dogma with the patent inferiority of foreigners and the subject races. 'I cannot help wondering why God created coloured people, seeing all the resultant difficulties caused thereby,' meditates one Christian. 'Adam and Eve were white,' declares another, 'so how did coloured races come into existence?' God does indeed move in mysterious ways, causing another Englishman to grumble, 'Why our all-wise Creator should have chosen such a distasteful – even disgusting – means of reproducing humanity is a thing I personally have never been able to understand.'

Naturally Englishmen have to be protected from this sort of thing, and they have officials to keep an eye on such subversive groups as Whitley Bay and Monkseaton Amateur Lyric Society, making them delete a Van Dam from their pantomime in favour of a Van Drat. Men of the calibre of Major

'Cockie' Harding de Fonblanque Cox, eighty-one, are appointed to scrutinize film scripts and promise 'no vulgarity. I shall judge film stories as I would horseflesh or a dog.'

Which brings us to the Englishman's love of animals, whether horses, dogs, cats, budgies, caterpillars or worms. He would save a snail from the perils of an air flight on a Comet from Nairobi, and take him for safety to an RSPCA hostel; he would suspend a shilling-a-tail campaign to exterminate squirrels in the mating season, for fear the young might starve in their nests; and if he shoots game he would like to be described as 'a merciful man who cherished the victims he slew so cleanly'.

The Englishman is reputed to have a great love of justice, though this is not always evident in a court of law. Courts are surrealist places, where anything can happen, where men take oaths on steak and kidney puddings, police superintendents summons themselves and plead guilty to the magistrates, pedestrians are ruled not to be vehicles, and 'an ordinary little case' is one in which a man is charged with 'indecency with four or five guardsmen'.

But the Englishman finds his true level in the day-to-day wisdom of council business. English councillors act with English pragmatism, and sometimes with Solomon-like inventiveness. They will have workmen take planks out of the seats of bus shelters and make holes in the walls so as to make life uncomfortable for the hooligans who have been wrecking them. Where nine parks compete for prizes, councillors will award them all the first prize, to avoid jealousy among the ratepayers. On carnival occasions they relax and become as other men, decorating floats, for example, to show the stages through which sewage passes.

Above all, the Englishman regards his class-system as the most precious jewel in England's crown, and will take great pains to ensure that it is maintained and registered in every facet of life – even the humblest. Only an Englishman could have classified the chamber pots on an admiralty stores list with such loving care:

'pots, chamber, plain,

pots, chamber, with admiralty monogram in blue for hospital use,

pots, chamber, fluted, with royal cypher in gold, for flag officers only,

pots, chamber, round, rubber, lunatic.'

Thus is the social order preserved.

1

The years before the war. But nobody wants to know that war is on the way, and they turn with pleasure to the achievements of Len Hutton, amassing a record Test score of 364 runs against the Australians at the Oval, or Sir Malcolm Campbell, outstripping everyone on land, hitting 300 m.p.h. for the first time. The big diversion is the Abdication scandal, as the man born to be King of England renounces all for a divorced American lady. By 1936 Neville Chamberlain has become Prime Minister and the war build-up is ominous. The Germans build the Siegfried Line. Beverley Nichols, a young man down from Oxford, who's been promised a brilliant writing career, looks on Hitler's better qualities and says: 'Herr Hitler has one of the endearing characteristics of Ferdinand the Bull. Just when the crowds expect him to be most violent he stops and smells the flowers. I have the feeling, and I hope I am right, that for the next month or so Herr Hitler is going to take things a little easier and smell the flowers and listen to the nightingales.' But Hitler ignores this good advice, and Britain goes to war over Poland on 3 September 1939.

□ In 1922 he was in Constantinople when things were very critical and they had a lot of trouble there. All sorts and conditions of nationalities were there armed to the teeth and not a night passed without some trouble and shouting and screaming. There were a few British soldiers there as military policemen who had nothing but side-arms, but they just walked up and gave the fellows a good kick on the shins or a jolt on the jaw and the whole thing was settled in five seconds, entirely due to the personality of the Englishmen. He had never had a better example of what English people could do in this world, as they were now doing in leading the world forward to that economic recovery which was beginning to take place under the leadership of the British race. *Speech at annual dinner reported in* HANTS AND SUSSEX NEWS

□ My knowledge of foreign languages is rather shaky, and they always seem to be harder to understand on the air except when an Englishman is speaking them. '*Our Wireless Correspondent*' *in the* EVENING NEWS

□ It used to be said that you could always spot an Englishman in cosmopolitan company by the way he wore his flannels. There is evidently a very high standard now throughout the Empire. EVENING NEWS

□ Memories of the Ghillies' Ball at the castle were recalled by Prince Nicholas. 'What impressed us so much was the extraordinary dignity of people belonging to such different classes. I don't think such a thing would be possible in any other country. It would engender familiarity, and that sort of thing.' STAR

□ Our Frontiers, bounded by the merciful sea, have, in His Goodness, been laid down by Almighty God, and they will remain fixed, immutable and inviolate, please the Lord!! until the end of Time. *Article in* SUNDAY PICTORIAL

□ It is recorded that there are only 75 Great Auk's eggs in existence. Great Britain owns 44, the United States 14, France 7, Germany 5, and Holland 2, while Denmark, Portugal and Switzerland own one each. It is gratifying to note that the six eggs sold yesterday were all acquired by British collectors. THE TIMES

□ A rapidly changing world regards with increasing admiration the wise conservatism of the Englishman and in no sphere is this more eloquently expressed than in his underwear. *Advertisement in* EVENING STANDARD

□ A broken knife was produced at Clerkenwell when two youths appeared before Mr Pope charged with shop-breaking. 'Why don't you buy a British knife?' Mr Pope asked them. 'You had better buy British if you are going in for burglary. This one is no earthly use!' *Report in daily paper*

□ For an English woman to marry a foreigner is an insult to her race. When will a law be passed to terminate this growing practice? *Letter in the* STAR

□ When God wants a hard thing done, He tells it to his Englishmen. *From the* ANTHOLOGY OF EMPIRE

□ I have a great personal admiration for Mussolini, who has welded a nation out of a collection of touts, blackmailers, ice-cream vendors, and gangsters. *Letter in the* SATURDAY REVIEW

□ Our English literature is the finest literature in the world and is worth the whole of Greek, Roman, French, German, American, Italian, Spanish, Chinese and Russian literature put together. AN ENGLISH COURSE FOR EVERY-BODY *by S. P. B. Mais*

□ When a white man laughs he means his laughter and regulates it. With the black race the contrary is the case. Both coal-black mammy and her male counterpart when they are tickled laugh too much, partly out of vanity and because of their superb teeth, and partly out of a mentality which when fully

Stop laughing you black devil!

pool, which is one of the biggest in the South of England, told the *Daily Herald*. 'Our experience is that women bathers, in particular, do not like to be in the pool at the same time as coloured men.' DAILY HERALD

☐ Moreover, in so far as he knows or cares anything about it at all, the average Briton entirely sympathizes with Italy's Abyssinian aims. Our history being what it is, we can hardly, unless we are a nation of case-hardened hypocrites, do otherwise. EVENING NEWS

☐ In a fortnight Britain will have none of her summer birds left. There will be only her own native birds that would rather risk death in the rigours of an English winter than singe under a foreign sun. SUNDAY EXPRESS

☐ From the British point of view the Cypriots have been too little conscious in the past of their membership of the British Empire. Permanent contact with the Imperial forces and the constant presence of British aeroplanes and warships would give them a different outlook. THE TIMES

☐ At the national festivals [in Spain] one is struck by the comely peasant girls, in all the bravery of their native finery, and the clean-looking stalwart lads dancing with them, and one realizes that here is first-class material for citizenship or cannon-fodder, but not for Bolshevism. *Letter in the* MORNING POST

☐ The air of St Moritz is conducive to gaiety: the slightest amount of alcoholic refreshment, when taken at a height of 5,000 ft, is apt to cause lightheadedness, but luckily the control of one's behaviour is a prerogative of the Britisher. DAILY MAIL

grown retains much of the child. That is why, when both must inhabit the same country, it is necessary for the whites to look after and care for the black. *James Agate in the* SUNDAY TIMES

☐ 'It is not a question of a colour bar in the accepted sense,' the manager of the

15

□ Other nations may sneer at the hypocritical English but only we can carry it off in the grand manner. DAILY SKETCH

□ Silver Cigarette Case, engraved with map of Europe, British Isles inlaid in Gold. *Advertisement in* PUNCH

□ They had interesting discussions, which broadened the mind, and anybody who believed in 'my country right or wrong' was welcome. MIDLAND DAILY TELEGRAPH

□ Active Englishman (50) with correct outlook, seeks work. *Advertisement in* THE TIMES

□ The truth is that no country in Europe but our own can conceive it is possible that action can be dictated by purely moral motives, entirely regardless of self-interest, and the sooner we recognize that we are the only country in Europe with a conscience the better ... we must recognize that our moral standpoint is beyond the comprehension of other European countries. *Letter in* THE TIMES

□ When Rudyard Kipling wrote his famous *Barrack-room Ballads* he put the whole philosophy of British rule in India into a single line of verse, 'You're a better man than I am, Gunga Din.' *Mr Sydney Carroll in* THE SUNDAY TIMES

□ Under its very roof, in the present coffee-room, King Richard III signed the death warrant of the Duke of Buckingham; who could fail to enjoy an excellent lunch in such Royal surroundings? *Remarks on the Angel Hotel at Grantham in the L.N.E.R.'s booklet,* RAILWAY AND ROAD-WAY HOLIDAYS (LINCOLNSHIRE AND THE DUKERIES)

□ Sir,
   Your correspondent, 'Springfield', asks: 'Why should Britain be called upon to "hold the baby" in every crisis which crops up?' May I take this opportunity to point out to him that this is the particular task that the Almighty has chosen Britain to perform? It is her duty to lead the nations to that World Utopia to which we are all striving. From 1800, Britain has grown into the mightiest Empire the world has ever known, and has taken the lead in world politics. *Letter in the* GLASGOW DAILY RECORD AND MAIL

The English are remarkable for the character and quality of their leaders

□ Many people are muddle-headed about armament firms. They think that they, for financial reasons, would welcome war. As a matter of fact wars are ruinous to armament firms. *Viscount Castlerosse in the* SUNDAY EXPRESS

□ A Sir Edward Gray denied a German report that captured French and British soldiers had been found with dum-dum bullets.

This favourite atrocity allegation in all modern wars is that the soldier cuts the nickel coating of his lead bullet, so that when it enters the body of the enemy it spreads horribly, instead of making a neat little hole. SUNDAY DESPATCH

□ In his speech at the *Sunday Times* Book Club yesterday Sir Austen Chamberlain maintained the old tradition that English statesmen are at their best when they talk about books. DAILY TELE-GRAPH

□ The Duke of Kent and Princess Marina are like captives fettered to the oars of fame, living in a smokescreen of limelight ... *Viscount Castlerosse in the* DAILY EXPRESS

□ At last Conservatives have grasped the importance of feminine good looks, Lady Janet Bailey (dark and handsome), Lady Diana Cooper (a miracle of loveliness), Lady Melchett (a golden page), Mrs Cunningham-Reid (classical and Titian) are helping tonight at the Steeplechase Ball – don't be misled, regulars, it has nothing to do with racing, it means a check on socialism! TATLER

□ I read with amazement the letter of Mrs Hilda Beale. If the working classes do not provide the country with a stock of miners, scavengers, bus drivers, sewermen, fishermen, dock labourers, etc., who is to do it? *Letter in the* DAILY TELEGRAPH

☐ Lord Derby, one of the most accomplished of after-dinner speakers, read his speech at last night's dinner to inaugurate the British Industries Fair . . . throwing his manuscript aside he paid tribute to the interest of the Royal Family in the Fair, remarking; 'Hour after hour they go round and round showing an honesty of purpose I should like many of my horses to have.' DAILY TELEGRAPH

☐ You will remember . . . that at an election in London not long ago we lost. It was lost very largely on a campaign which reflected little credit on those who engaged in it – a campaign of peace. I do not think there is a worse sign of the times than that a sacred subject of that kind should be dragged down into the political arena. *Mr Baldwin, reported in the* DAILY TELEGRAPH

☐ The Government move forward slowly, but as quickly as they know how. For them to move forward more rapidly without further knowledge would mean moving back at a faster rate than the rate of going forward – the method of procedure in many other countries. *Isidore Ostrer in the* SUNDAY REFEREE

☐ The Scout movement teaches you to be good citizens, and not know anything about politics. *Rover Scout explaining the aims of the movement.*

☐ It is idle . . . to talk of the wickedness of killing, because if and when the next war comes men will think only of the nobleness of dying. *Lord Chief Justice (Lord Hewart) opening a Territorial*

Drill-hall, reported in the WESTERN MAIL

☐ The bows of the *Napier Star* had ripped through the bows of the *Laurentic* just beneath one of the anchors . . .
Three men were found dead in their bunks, three others were missing, their bodies hidden amongst the tangled mass of debris. . . .
How near disaster came to catastrophe was also evident. Had the *Napier Star* struck twenty yards further astern, she would have cut clean into the first-class staterooms. DAILY MAIL

☐ Chatsworth without the Duchess of Devonshire would still be beautiful, but I do not stand alone in believing that the trees would hold their heads less high and the flowers lose something of their radiance. STAR

☐ The value of the unemployed is more important than ages and numbers. In my opinion it requires two million as a safety-valve to prevent strikes. *Letter in the* WESTERN MORNING NEWS

☐ Well, maybe my news-sense is all wrong, but it seems to me that when the possessor of one of the oldest baronetcies marries his deceased wife's sister it savours of half a column. *Lord Donegall in the* SUNDAY DISPATCH

☐ It is characteristic of a Party that has not shrunk from opposing the Speaker in his constituency that it should also have dragged foreign affairs into the forefront of its election platform. *Leader in the* MORNING POST

☐ Sir Paul Dukes, who wrote the Gossip here a few weeks ago, spent the week-end with me recently. As we walked across the lawn he got down on his hands, cocked his legs up into the air, and continued to walk beside me. Apparently one must keep fit in the Intelligence Service. *Provincial paper*

□ What should the British attitude be? This can best be decided by NOTING WHAT THE SOVIET WOULD HAVE THIS COUNTRY DO AND TAKING THE OPPOSITE COURSE. *Leader in the* DAILY MAIL

□ In order that she may play her part to perfection in the Viceregal life of India, Lady Linlithgow, who sails with her husband, the new Viceroy, very soon, has spent 100 hours before a mirror in a West End fitting-room. It has taken Lady Linlithgow and her dressmaker five months to evolve her magnificent wardrobe. DAILY TELEGRAPH

□ Captain R. G. Briscow, M.P. for Cambridgeshire, speaking at a bowls dinner in Cambridge, said: 'If only Hitler and Mussolini could have a good game of bowls once a week at Geneva, I feel that Europe would not be as troubled as it is.' BIRMINGHAM POST

□ A minor point, which many may consider a very major one, is that the handing back without reference to the resident population would not be in accordance with English principles of equity. ... But we do not really know Native opinion. After some careful propaganda it would appear to be worth the risk of taking a referendum throughout the country after making sure that it would go, overwhelmingly, in England's favour. UGANDA GUARDIAN

□ COUNTRY ON SIDE OF FRANCO
Mr P. Dunne, M.P. for Stalybridge and Hyde, told a *Daily Despatch*

representative last night how he and four Conservative M.P. companions found the Franco-controlled part of Spain so quiet that it was 'like travelling in England.... We met General Franco. I think he is a very nice man. He is a keen golfer, with a handicap of 2. He is received with great enthusiasm wherever he appears.' DAILY DESPATCH

□ He [the Duke of Norfolk] hunts regularly on blood-stock horses of his own choosing and breeding, and once showed a surprising sense of humour by flicking a pat of butter on to a screen at a dinner party. CAVALCADE

□ What a pleasant thing it would be if all those people earning £2,000 and over a year would each adopt an unemployed man and help him to preserve his sense of proportion by sending him an

occasional cheerful letter or an old book. *Letter in the* NEWS CHRONICLE

☐ The cinema ... serves the proletariat as well as the middle classes. So long as we have the cinema and commercialized football, the proletariat will give no trouble to their masters in England. *Rev. J. C. Hardwick at the Conference of Modern Churchmen, reported in the* MORNING POST

☐ Atticus should have no politics, and therefore it is merely as an observer and not as a politician that he remarks that there is something impressive about the Conservative Party *en masse*. There is an indestructible atmosphere, a solidity which gives the comfort of permanency to the troubled mind. There is also a magnificence which survives in an age when sombreness is counted a virtue. I liked the tiaras and the medals and the sashes and the uniforms. *Atticus in the* SUNDAY TIMES

☐ If ever I wanted rough work done quickly and cheaply, give me the tramp navvy. Sub him every night, pay him a penny or two over the local rate, put a proper ganger over him, and you can work him sixteen hours a day. *Article in the* COUNTRYMAN

☐ It has repeatedly been officially denied that bombing breeds resentment. *J. A. Chamier, Secretary-General of the Air League of the British Empire, in the* MANCHESTER GUARDIAN

☐ Real prosperity is abroad in the land. Good times are here. But those who are plunged in gloom will not believe it. ... The net sale of the *Daily Express* last week was 2,446,000 copies, the largest net sale we have ever known. *Lord Beaverbrook in the* DAILY EXPRESS

☐ When Arthur Balfour launched his scheme for peopling Palestine with Jewish immigrants, I am credibly informed that he did not know that there were Arabs in the country. *Dean Inge in* the EVENING STANDARD

☐ One of the first results of the pact with Eire is that Mr Neville Chamberlain will go fishing in Galway as soon as the House rises in July. SUNDAY DISPATCH

☐ One result of the cession of the Sudeten Areas of Czechoslovakia to Germany is that Roderich Menzel, the leading lawn tennis player of Czechoslovakia, will be available to Germany for Davis Cup matches. GLASGOW EVENING NEWS

☐ Mr A. P. Iliffe, chairman of the Oxford Ratepayers' Association, spoke for Mr Lindsay. 'Although I am a Conservative,' he said, 'this time I am going to think for myself.' *Provincial paper.*

☐ Colonel L. Tebbutt, an alderman of the Cambridgeshire County Council, opposed the amendment [to give employees a week's holiday with pay]. He said that for the first fifteen years of his career he did not have a holiday and he could not for the life of him see why working men should have any holidays at all. ... The amendment was a backdoor method of getting higher wages for the men, without anybody knowing about it. It was decided not to include Good Friday as a holiday as 'everywhere amusements were closed and the men did not know what to do with themselves and were best at work'. *Press report of meeting of the River Great Ouse Catchment Board, at Cambridge*

☐ It did not matter to brawny Owen Simpson, unemployed joiner, that the tall boy who stood in his path and tried to save a goal was P. A. D. Crichton, son of Sir George Crichton, former Comptroller of the King's Household. He shot straight and true and scored the goal which equalized the teams – two all after extra time. DAILY SKETCH

☐ People need not be surprised at a good deal of sleeping going on in the House of Commons, said Sir George Hume, M.P., at a meeting last night at Greenwich, which he has represented since 1922. 'You get weary at times, and in the atmosphere of the House it is very difficult to keep awake,' he said. 'But the public do not seem to be able to appreciate our difficulties. Some of the best Members are the silent ones.' DAILY TELEGRAPH

☐ Like Bunyan's *Pilgrim's Progress*, Hitler's *Mein Kampf* was written in gaol and is worthy to be ranked with it. Hitler's motto appears to be, 'Love your neighbour better than yourself.' *Letter in the* YORKSHIRE POST

☐ But we cannot understand why, although there are thousands of women and girls unemployed, when we ask at the labour exchanges for domestic servants we are told that none is available. I, for example, who live alone very quietly with a staff of seven domestics, am quite unable to obtain a kitchenmaid. *Letter in* THE TIMES

☐ Mr Ernest Brown crystallized the unemployment problem when he told Parliament that it was really a question of finding jobs. OXFORD MAIL

☐ If we provide money for mental hospitals the chances are that we shall get more mental cases, and if we provide more and more money for unemployment we shall get more unemployed. EVENING STANDARD

☐ I am certain that the world needs contrast and the slums supply it. *Rachel Ferguson in* PASSIONATE KENSINGTON

☐ It is now becoming plain that Franco is not the devil he was painted, nor are the Spanish Moors, who fought for him, anything but great gentle giants, who felt infinitely hurt at the thought that their dusky faces should be used to scare the more ignorant people whom the socialists could influence. EAST HAM PATRIOT

☐ A Conservative Government can change its policy completely and still remain in office. The Socialist Party will never expand till the minds of its leaders become as elastic. DAILY EXPRESS

☐ 'What has shocked us in this country,' he said, 'is that these Indian leaders have thought fit to use the international situation in order to promote a further step towards self-government.' *Report of the Marquess of Salisbury's speech in Parliament in the* DAILY TELEGRAPH

☐ Stalin's vision won for him the leadership of the Bolshevik Party. This vision, as we saw at the beginning, is based on a fundamental respect of the opinions of others. DAILY WORKER

☐ Shall we send Lady Diana Duff Cooper to be the First Lady of the Admiralty? After all, she would know her way about, for her husband used to be First Lord. I once met Diana wearing a yachting cap while travelling on a

French train. This shows that the sea is in her blood. WOMAN'S JOURNAL

☐ The Blackshirt movement is not an army. It is not a political movement that expects to attain its ends by other than political means. It has nothing whatever to do with Fascists or Nazis. EVENING NEWS

☐ Before the organization of the Blackshirt movement free speech did not exist in this country. *Sir Oswald Mosley*

☐ Remarkable scenes were witnessed at Linz, where great mass meetings awaited Hitler's arrival. Armoured cars rattled over the cobbled streets as 300 warplanes zoomed overhead.

When it was announced at one of the meetings that Mr Ward Price, of the *Daily Mail*, had arrived, cheering went on for nearly a minute. In broken German, Mr Price congratulated Austria on her 'hour of happiness'. REYNOLDS NEWS

☐ Herr Hitler has one of the endearing characteristics of Ferdinand the Bull. Just when the crowds expect him to be most violent he stops and smells the flowers. I have a feeling, and I hope I am right, that for the next month or so Herr Hitler is going to take things a little easier and smell the flowers and listen to the nightingales.

Our policy should be to encourage him to go on developing the aesthetic side of his nature. *Beverley Nichols in the* SUNDAY GRAPHIC

☐ Now that the Royal Standard is flying over Buckingham Palace again London reassumes its 'settled' look. It is a psychological fact that London never really 'feels itself' when the King and Queen are away; their Majesties' return makes everybody feel at home. DAILY MAIL

☐ The Duke received everywhere a typical Bush welcome. From the trees beside the road bell-birds sang their tuneful notes, and there were occasional hilarious outbursts from laughing-jackasses. THE TIMES

☐ The House of Lords has lost, at the age of 91, one of its most picturesque personalities in the Earl of Morton. He had a great gift for silence, and during all the years that he attended at Westminster as a Scottish representative Peer his voice was never heard in debate. THE TIMES

Surely everyone knows that the most remarkable thing about this great Empire is the fact that nearly all of our overseas possessions literally fell into our lap, and in many cases were acquired with the greatest reluctance. *Major-General L. C. Dunsterville, in a letter to the* ROYAL CENTRAL ASIAN SOCIETY JOURNAL

What of the English people themselves?

□ While sex prejudices still exist in other departments, there is no trace of it in Somerset House. There is complete equality between the sexes, except in pay. SUNDAY EXPRESS

□ Wanted young girl lavatory attendant, genial work. WESTERN DAILY PRESS AND BRISTOL MIRROR

□ One afternoon in Arran I saw ten fairies playing out and in among gorse bushes and round about the grazing sheep. The sheep were quite undisturbed except that if a fairy went too near one of them it would trot off a few yards. *Letter in* JOHN O'LONDON'S WEEKLY

□ On going to bed at night the hair should be brushed thoroughly, arranged comfortably and carefully in case of a burglar, a fireman or a policeman. They are all men, too, you know, and should be considered. DAILY SKETCH

□ Then the population of 45 will adjourn to the village hall to drink the health of the King in ale. Port wine will be supplied to those who are teetotallers, in accordance with a well-known English custom. THE TIMES

□ Public conveniences erected in the Abbey for Coronation Day reflect neatly the quaint distinctions of British social life. Those of the male sex will be marked: Peers, Gentlemen, Men; while others will be labelled; Peeresses, Ladies, Women. DAILY MIRROR

□ There is no such thing as a household drudge in South Africa. Even in the poorest farms or in the meanest suburb, there is a native to do the work of the home. He will start at half-past five or six in the morning, and if he is well trained he will not only do all the cleaning and tidying in the house, but he will cook all the meals, and perhaps find time to launder or garden. DAILY TELEGRAPH

☐ Mr Walter Eliot (Secretary for Scotland) caused some surprise when discussing the suggestion that surplus herrings should be made available to the poor at prices lower than those charged in the shops. There was nothing the unemployed would resent more than being used as a dumping ground for food products. NEWS CHRONICLE

☐ GLORIOUS WINTER CLIMATE — Superbly designed house in most exclusive all-the-year-round beauty spot. Semi-tropical climate; typical Continental atmosphere; social life of high standard; exceptional golf and tennis; 4 bedrooms, double reception, etc, central heating; garage; gardens; suitable week-end home (only 90 min. London), or otherwise. Angmering-on-Sea. *Advertisement in the* SUNDAY TIMES

☐ A warning of the dangerous effects attendant on the indiscriminate use of the drug benzedrine is given by the British Medical Journal. The habitual use of the drug, even in small doses, has been observed in some cases to involve 'a dangerous degree of disrespectfulness to superior officers on telephones'. DAILY TELEGRAPH

☐ A middle-aged man rowing on Regent's Park lake tried to stand in his skiff for the Two Minutes' Silence. He overbalanced, fell, and stood waist-deep in water to keep the Silence. DAILY MIRROR

☐ One scene in *The Women* shows a lying-in hospital. Objection is taken to this scene by the Lord Chamberlain's department on the grounds that a woman gives vent to expressions of tedium at the prospect of becoming a mother. EVENING STANDARD

☐ On Wednesday the Westminster Coroner referred to the suicide of Major Rowlandson, of Kenley, Surrey, who shot himself within a few minutes of the time when his insurance policy lapsed, as a 'cold-blooded method to defraud the company'. NEWS CHRONICLE

☐ My nephew aged two has a head of curls which accurately forecast the weather. When they are tightly coiled rain always follows, when they relax into fine silken strands a spell of fine weather can be expected. *Letter in the* SUNDAY EXPRESS

☐ When Putney becomes precarious, where on earth is stability to be looked for? OBSERVER

☐ For a long time I used as my sanctuary the words: 'This, too, will pass,' and they never once failed to prove themselves true. . . . Do you worry? Try not to. . . . Lie still on you back; think of your body as a row of pebbles, and drop them one by one into a pond. DAILY SKETCH

☐ Never wear shoes or a wrist-watch if you want to be successful in business. They are too effeminate. Try a pocket watch and boots for a change, and notice the difference in your earning power. *Letter in the* DAILY MIRROR

☐ Owing to a girl's bashfulness, Brighton is without a Lady Godiva for its Jubilee Pageant today.
A last-minute effort is being made by the organizers to find a girl willing to

take the part. Otherwise, the white horse will be ridden by a man wearing flesh-coloured tights and a wig of flowing golden hair. DAILY TELEGRAPH

□ Generally, he said, he considered that the flogging he saw was not brutal. There was a table covered with first-aid material, the doctor was there, and, after the flogging, the prisoner 'is swathed like a wounded man in battle'. *Hon. Edward Cadogan reported in the* DAILY TELEGRAPH

□ I believe in Stiff Collars on ethical and national grounds. They are a bulwark against lawlessness. *From* THE GROCER'S HANDBOOK

□ Even diet can be fixed by the stars.
'It need not be monotonous, for though Sunday's star might indicate dry toast and soda water, Wednesday's star might order roast duck and green peas. DAILY MAIL

□ Georgie: 'Will you please tell me the correct way to eat grapes and bananas?'
'I have always eaten grapes by picking the fruit from the stem, conveying them to my mouth with my fingers, and removing pips by ejecting them into the hollow of my hands.' DAILY MIRROR

Women have their own special problems

☐ Heaps of women come to me with their nails cracked right across; they ask me to repair the damage, and I tell them that they simply must give them a rest. This is possible by going without liquid polish when they are week-ending in the country. I know it takes a little courage to be the only woman with naked nails, but believe me, it's worth it. VOGUE

☐ Look at the beauty of your thighs, at the classic curves of your legs, as they taper and taper just as the stems of a flower.

THERE CAN BE NO SELF-DECEPTION BETWEEN YOU AND YOURSELF WHEN YOU ARE STANDING IN THE NUDE.

You see yourself as God made you. You can't help but be awed by the beauty of His work. DAILY MIRROR

□ If a woman wishes to be really smart this winter she must wear a coloured ring on the small toe of her left foot to match the colour of the nail varnish she uses on her fingers. YORKSHIRE TELEGRAPH AND STAR

□ Jubilee is the catchword of the season. Jubilee coiffures, jubilee dresses, jubilee jewellery, and now jubilee finger nails. The pattern is a patriotic one of red, white and blue stripes, surmounted with a gold crown. This elaborate design is made by stencils. One side of the nail is painted blue, the other red, and a golden crown is stencilled on top. It is correct to have only the index finger or thumb mounted with this design. KENSINGTON NEWS

□ Many of England's beauty parlours are observing the period of national mourning by putting lotions, scents and powders in black glass containers. And a nation wearing black, white, purple and lavender has changed the trend in make-up, too, with a decided fashion for violet eye-shadow, and powders with a tendency to give a pale, delicate look. *Fashion paper*

□ Unlike so many women who see in themselves nothing more than a logical, biological necessity, Princess von Bismarck is charmingly excited at being a woman. SUNDAY TIMES

Morality is a question of serious concern

☐ A thirty-three-year-old married man, found guilty of an assault on a school-girl, has been sentenced to two months' imprisonment and castration ... the man has, it is stated, willingly consented to the operation (which tends to have a definite curative effect). EVERYMAN

☐ Let us then start a movement: I will call it 'Back to the gooseberry bush', and I shall expect all my followers to take an oath to give as little information as they truthfully can to the young and to leave the most mysterious things of life steeped in the awe and dignity which naturally belongs to them. *Article in the* SUNDAY DISPATCH

☐ The Bishop of London said that a vast trade was being done in contraceptives. He would like to make a bonfire of them and dance round it. *Report of House of Lords debate*

☐ 'The book deals,' said the Attorney-General, 'with what everybody will recognize as an unsavoury subject – gratification of sexual appetite.' DAILY SKETCH

☐ The marriage was a happy one, except that the wife refused cohabitation. MANCHESTER GUARDIAN

☐ Surprise has been caused all along the south coast by a bathing innovation at Bognor Regis, Sussex – the issuing of a double ticket by which a husband and wife may share a bathing hut at the same time. At no other resort is such a practice permitted. EVENING NEWS

☐ If only men could love each other like dogs, the world would be a paradise. *James Douglas in the* SUNDAY EXPRESS

☐ I am twenty-nine, single; I neither drink nor smoke. I do not seem to be able to overcome the sex impulse. Is this due to catarrh, and will a diet of vegetables and salads help to abate it? *Letter in* HEALTH FOR ALL

☐ A move to extend the hours of Sunday bathing at North Berwick Swimming Pond from 2 p.m. to 5 p.m. was defeated at a meeting of the Town Council last night. Provost Eeles, who seconded, expressed the opinion that Sunday afternoon bathing at North Berwick pond would lead to the ruination of the town. EDINBURGH EVENING NEWS

☐ The bride's father is proprietor of an old-fashioned meat business ... the bride wore a gown of white satin fashioned with short leg-of-mutton sleeves and worn with long kid gloves. YORKSHIRE EVENING POST

☐ Dr Stephenson said he would not punish sex perverts. He would say to them: 'I hope you will have a better time in another world, but we cannot keep you in this,' and then he would put them in a lethal chamber. SUNDAY EXPRESS

☐ Dear Miss Dix,
  My fiancé and I found your article 'If Hitler married Mae West', very instructive and helpful. We feared that we might not be able to get on in married life. After reading what you wrote, we feel we have a better chance of happiness when we marry at Easter. *Letter in the* DAILY MIRROR

☐ It is a record Bank Holiday for marriage masquerading. All over Britain, in seaside hotels, in country inns, young lovers, posing as man and wife, are together.

Proof is in the record sales of sixpenny wedding rings – 80 per cent of the buyers being girls, most of them blushingly making all types of excuses about the purchase of a sixpenny 'ticket' to bliss.

Comment of the manager of a chain jewellery store was: 'The demand for wedding rings has been ten times greater this week than at any other time of the year. It is always the same at August Bank Holiday.' SUNDAY PICTORIAL

☐ 'It's a miracle – an act of God,' says Councillor Thomas Daly, seventy-eight-years old purity campaigner of Cobham (Surrey) who has become the father of the baby boy with whom you see him and his wife in this picture. 'We prayed for a baby and here it is,' he added. 'We shall pray again – I want another.' DAILY MIRROR

☐ P.L. No, it is not possible for 'two devout Catholic girls' who are 'very much in love with one another' to have 'a matrimonial service'. The Church's matrimonial service is restricted to those who, in accordance with God's holy institution, choose a partner of the opposite sex. Are there no eligible young men in your parish? UNIVERSE

The administration of the country is in the safe hands of the Law

□ On the right of the platform is the old jury box, in which the jury is literally impanelled, so constructed that it can be shut up into the wall when not required for use. *Extract from the* OFFICIAL HANDBOOK *of Sandwich*

□ When a woman complained to the Willesden magistrate that her husband gave her no money, but only kept her, the magistrate said there was no law to make a husband give his wife money. All he could be compelled to do was to provide her with a home and reasonable food and clothing. The wife: Then he can take another woman out with his money and give me none? The magistrate: That is the law. *Report in daily paper.*

□ He pleaded that justice would be met if the summonses were dismissed on payment of costs, as a conviction might count against his clients in their future life. Supporting this plea, Mr David Thomas said the seven defendants were all University or public-school men. MANCHESTER GUARDIAN

□ A solicitor declined to go any further with his defence in a street-betting case at Liverpool yesterday when the police produced photographs of the incidents alleged. 'I think the police go beyond all bounds,' he said. 'When they bring photographs here. What chance does it give a struggling advocate?' MORNING POST

□ Walter Ednam, 21, an unemployed green-grocer's assistant, of Ashbourne Road, Mitcham, was at Croydon sentenced to three months' hard labour for fraudulently using electricity at a telephone kiosk at Mitcham. It was stated that he called up the operator, addressed her as 'my dear', said he did not want any number, and left the box without paying. DAILY TELEGRAPH

☐ When a 60-year-old labourer was found guilty at Derbyshire Quarter Sessions, at Derby, yesterday, of stealing coal valued at 6d. from a local pit, the foreman of the jury intimated that the women members desired to recommend him to mercy. The chairman, Mr H. St John Raikes, K.C., asked them to give a reason, and when none was forthcoming, he said it was difficult to understand such a recommendation.

'Year by year,' he said, 'since women have been serving, a certain amount of sickly sentimentality has been shown. Unless there is some strong reason, they should be chary of making recommendations. It is rather a slight on the Court.'

He sentenced the man to six months' hard labour. OBSERVER

☐ A man was charged at Sheffield Police Court yesterday with using obscene language to a clockwork mouse which refused to perform on the pavement. MANCHESTER GUARDIAN

☐ Mr T. Springer, who defended, said it could not be held that a man committed a criminal offence when he was not aware what he was doing. Before a man could be driving dangerously he must be wide awake. EVENING STANDARD

☐ 'We can't build warships and things like that unless you people pay up more cheerfully,' said Alderman Barber in dealing with fifty-six income-tax defaulters at Wood Green Court to-day. EDINBURGH EVENING DISPATCH

☐ 'I do not know whether you are a knave or a fool if you thought you were going to corrupt a police officer with a paltry £5,' said Mr Herbert Metcalfe, the Magistrate at Old-street. DAILY TELEGRAPH

☐ Mr Alfred Dennis, J.P., will celebrate his 97th birthday next week by retiring from business. He has been in the drapery business of Dennis and Company, Weymouth, since 1863. When he was 94 he resigned from the chairmanship of the Weymouth Bench owing to defective hearing. But he said to-day that after he had retired from business he intended to return to the Bench. EVENING NEWS

A powerful cultural heritage and educational tradition

□ Word has gone to officials in the light entertainment department of the BBC that there must be stricter censorship of variety broadcasts. Complaints have been made that unnecessarily broad jokes and strong language have got past the microphone ... in future 'Damn,' 'Hell!' and 'Blast' are to be excised from the plays. EVENING STANDARD

□ If for no other reason than sheer bulk this book has to be taken seriously. OBSERVER

□ Wagner was an artist, but he was by no means so artistic as all that. On the contrary, he was actively engaged at this time in a love affair with a married lady. SUNDAY REFEREE

□ The novel has a quality of sharp and vivid actuality which continually brings to mind familiar passages of Icelandic poetry. THE TIMES LITERARY SUPPLEMENT

□ I hate harrowing plays. *Love On the Dole* made me cry with rage – to think that one of the greatest of arts had been used to upset people so. *Evelyn Millard, woman dramatist in an interview in* THE ERA

□ The Astaire–Rogers combination holds the stage most of the time, but there is room for a newcomer of charm, Harriet Hilliard, who sings 'Get Thee Behind me – ' (the 'Satan' has been cut by the British Board of Film Censors). EVENING STANDARD

□ Major Harding de Fonblanque Cox, known to intimates as 'Cockie', appointed at the age of eighty-one by Lord Tyrell, film censor, to act as assistant reader of scripts, raised a warning finger. He said: 'I SHALL PRESERVE A PERFECTLY OPEN MIND; BUT I WILL NOT COUNTENANCE VULGARITY. NO, MY BOY, LET US SHOW CLEAN FILMS IN THE OLD COUNTRY.' His enthusiasm grew as he continued, 'I shall judge film stories as I would horseflesh or a dog. I shall look for clean lines. The same critical faculties with which I think I am gifted in the show ring will be brought to bear in my new task.' SUNDAY EXPRESS

□ The novel is a special English responsibility, since, despite all distortions of hypocrisy, the English race has realized and established a pattern of sexual happiness which has not otherwise existed in the world. *Mr Basil de Selincourt in the* OBSERVER

□ An even better index of national recovery and optimism than dry statistics is to be found in the salerooms. When men are poor and frightened they will not buy Rembrandt etchings and Italian majolica. OBSERVER

□ My own personal reaction is that most ballets would be quite delightful if it were not for the dancing. EVENING STANDARD

□Mr Alexander Korda has by this film shown to the whole world that naturalized Englishmen can direct films better than anybody else. *Viscount Castlerosse in the* SUNDAY EXPRESS

□ On Saturday the programme returned to normal, but a typical BBC action was to 'vet' the dance music titles lest any of these be construed as having any bearing on the abdication crisis. ... From Ambrose's late night broadcast on Saturday, for instance, the following numbers were struck out by BBC orders: No Regrets, Crazy With Love, I Don't Want to Get Hot, and We Go Well Together. A general ban was imposed on the number, Front Page News. MELODY MAKER

□ Whitley Bay and Monkseaton Amateur Lyric Society's script for their annual pantomine was returned yesterday by the Lord Chancellor's department, to which all such scripts, amateur or professional, must go before production. One of the characters in the show, which is to be 'Dick Whittington', is, or rather was, named Van Dam. The censor requests that the name be altered to Van Drat. MANCHESTER GUARDIAN

□ A fashionable audience – with Queen Mary in a stage box, roared with laughter at the Haymarket Theatre,

London, last night as Dame Marie Tempest closed the first act of her new play, *Mary Goes to See*, with the words 'Obviously a —' (what the dictionary calls the female of the canine kind or opprobriously a woman).

The line was the biggest laugh of the play. DAILY EXPRESS

□ Happily, in a week more full of alarms and excursions than any other since the Great War, we had an example of the British spirit at its best.

Mr James Whitehead, 'cellist of the Philharmonic Trio, faced with one of those impossible modern foreign compositions which delight highbrows, said: 'Oh, I can't play this thing,' and walked off the platform. SUNDAY PICTORIAL

□ For my own part, I have always found it significant and interesting that the greatest musical nations in the world, the Germans and Italians, have both adopted the same form of Government.

What is the explanation: I am at a loss to understand it. *Lord Rothermere in the* DAILY MAIL

□ Some years ago I produced a dramatic sketch for a local Band of Hope entertainment. One of the characters was a Cockney obviously of the gutter-merchant type, into whose mouth the author had no doubt unthinkingly put many of the expressions to which I have referred. Luckily I thought of a way out of the difficulty. Whenever, for example, the word 'blimey' was used to convey extreme surprise, I substituted the words 'How odd!' I can truthfully say that the audience found these substitutions just as amusing as the expletives which the author had supplied, and which I myself thought highly objectionable. Could not the BBC Variety programmes be kept on the same high level without any loss of entertainment value? *Letter in the* RADIO TIMES

□ If you are a bad painter, not even the wealth of the Indies can get your picture into the Royal Academy. EVENING STANDARD

□ Opposing a proposal to name new roads in Great Yarmouth after Byron, Chaucer, Milton, Shakespeare and Tennyson, Mr R. F. Kerrison declared at Yarmouth Town Council today: 'In my opinion, the moral character of these people is not such that we should name new roads after them.' He suggested that the roads should be named after present councillors. DAILY MIRROR

□ The Rt Hon. Neville Chamberlain's authentic and copyright book of speeches *In Search of Peace* specially authorized by the Prime Minister and only available to old and new members of The National Book Association. The National Book Association was founded in 1937 to give its members important new books that have a sound, moderate and non-revolutionary aspect – N.B. The next choice is Hitler's *Mein Kampf*. *Advertisement in the* DAILY TELE-GRAPH

□ Our Prime Minister carries a pocket Shakespeare with him whenever he travels. He put Shakespeare on the map with a quotation from Henry IV when he set out for the Münich conference. SHEFFIELD STAR

□ Ordering the boy to be sent to an approved school for three years, the chairman, Col. F. G. Barker, said: 'What a dreadful commentary on modern education and religion. If he were at Eton he would be flogged out of his life.' STAR

□ The great moment came when the umpire, W. A. J. West, one of the most famous umpires of all times, could not be found for the group. 'Where's West?' we asked. 'He's gone west,' swiftly retorted Mr Stocks, maintaining the highest traditions of Uppingham humour. DAILY MAIL

□ Queen Elizabeth, who has a natural equipment of dignity, friendliness and charm of manner, is a great reader, and keeps well abreast of what is happening in the literary world. Her taste is for biography and travel, rather than for fiction. But this, perhaps is natural, since she has, as a very small girl at school, won prizes for literature and essay writing; and at the age of fourteen she passed the Junior Oxford examination. Hence, it is only appropriate that she should be an Hon. D.C.L. of Oxford, and an Hon. LL.D. of the Universities of Belfast, Glasgow and St Andrews. LANDMARK

□ Mr A. F. Boissier, who has just been appointed Headmaster of Harrow ... explained. 'We are a conservative school and I am a conservative man. I see no necessity for any important changes. Times may change, conditions may change, but the schoolboy remains the same for ever.' Thus has the zealot of 1919 mellowed with the years. SUNDAY TIMES

Religious heads keep an eye on the spiritual life of the community

□ The Pope paid a glowing tribute to artillerymen today when he received in audience 4,000 members of the National Ex-Artillerymen's Association, who had returned from their national conference at Naples. 'Artillery,' said the Pope, 'remains one of the learned arms, which demands not only special physical qualities, but also qualities of spirituality and intelligence.' DAILY EXPRESS

□ *C.I.D.* (Playhouse) by the Rev. William Haslam, Vicar of Brockenhurst. This is probably the best play ever written by a Vicar of Brockenhurst. SPHERE

□ Patron of vacant living in East Anglia invites recommendations. Net value about £530, large rectory and grounds. Primary qualification, capacity to be guide, philosopher and friend to agricultural people, for which in this case gentle birth essential. Open mind towards Bishop Barnes, birth control and psychic research secondary but helpful. *Advertisement in* THE TIMES

□ Anxious to hear their grievances the Bishop of London invited 16 unemployed dockers to tea with him at Fulham Palace.

They produced their balance sheets showing that they received only 5d. a day and 2d. for each child.

'So I produced my balance sheet,' said the Bishop at Bournemouth yesterday, 'which showed that I received £10,000 and my expenditure was £10,600.' NEWS CHRONICLE

□ A vicar, in the Infantry, 1914–19, longs to regain the spirit of the trenches by building a Church Hall in a suburb. THE TIMES

□ There are things in men's lives in peaceful England today which are far more horrible than a good, clean war. *Rev. N. G. Railton, Senior Chaplain to the Forces at Tidworth.* THE TIMES

□ Barriers between age and youth disappear in this spiritual army. Brig.-General P. Winder, D.S.O., trainer of racehorses and Great War veteran, describes himself as a 'recruit in this new enlistment'. 'I have tried pig-sticking, war and racing,' he says, 'but this Oxford Group game of changing the world is the most thrilling thing I have ever met.' DAILY RECORD

□ The portion of the carpet where the Throne stood and the King knelt at the Coronation ceremony in Westminster Abbey has been bought for Winchester Cathedral, and will be placed in the Sanctuary. The following are extracts from letters to the Dean of Winchester from the Office of Works:
'Your carpet is even more interesting than my previous letter foreshadowed. You will find on it some slight red marks; the two side by side represent the positions where stood the chairs occupied by the King and Queen in front of the Royal box. The third mark indicates the position of the stool where the King knelt during the Communion Service. Most interesting of all, in the opposite corner of the carpet stood the Throne. Its position is not indicated by any mark, but I think that you will be able to trace, even at this date, the imprints of the feet of the Throne.' THE TIMES

□ Being asked the way to the Workhouse by a needy looking man, I gave him a shilling. Judge of my surprise, as a local preacher and lifelong teetotaller, when he turned into the next 'pub' into which I followed in a useless effort to get my money back. What were my legal rights? *Letter in* JOHN BULL

□ We believe that Crockford's may now be reckoned amongst the National Institutions which have raised our country to the proud pre-eminence which it has long enjoyed and are believed to be at once the envy and despair of the rest of the civilized world. *From the preface to* CROCKFORD'S CLERICAL DIRECTORY *for 1937*

□ These books [of the Bible] were written over a long period of time. It took God longer to write the Bible than it has taken Him to build the British Empire. MODERN EVANGELISM *by William C. Macdonald*

□ May I, through your valuable *Cycling* ask Clubmen identified with the Oxford Group if they would kindly communicate with me. My vision is Christian Revolution through cycling to build a New England and a New World. *Letter in* CYCLING

□ Other writers say flogging is un-Christian, yet I seem to remember that Christ made a whip of small cords and drove the money-changers from the Temple, merely because they were cheating in unsuitable surroundings. There is nothing to tell us that these money-changers had been guilty of personal violence. *Letter in* THE TIMES

□ 'It is presumption on the part of humans to estimate whether Heaven is gaining or losing by a person's death,' said Councillor Ayley at the Walton and Weybridge Council Meeting, when a recommendation of its Burial Grounds Committee was rejected. The committee had refused the wish of a widow for the inscription she desired on a memorial stone to her husband in Weybridge cemetery. The wording which led to the controversy was: 'Our loss, Heaven's gain; one of the best the world contained.' EVENING STANDARD

□ The popular account of King John's financial dealing with Jewry is that he imprisoned wealthy Hebrews and had their teeth extracted in instalments until they yielded to his extortions. In all this, however, there are extenuations of King John. The Government had to be maintained out of royal patrimony. There was then no comprehensive and well-ordered system of rates and taxes. Nor did he deprive them of the means of livelihood or cause them to be 'beaten up'. His tooth-drawing was not sadistic, but a practical and comparatively mild way of exercising financial pressure. There was nothing malicious or destructive in it. CHURCH TIMES

□ TODAY'S QUESTION
People in Henley have objected to a local curate training to be a ballet-dancer, with the object of dancing in the Henley 'Ballet Circle'. As a result he has resigned from the Circle. Do you see any objection to a curate acting in this way? DAILY MIRROR

From the rites of the church it is a short step to the rules of cricket

□ It is not the mere presence of the clergy at Lord's that is impressive, but rather the twin stamp of English and Anglican which they bear. You can be sure that they are cricketers all, and because cricket is of the very soul of England it is in England's Church that they have found their vocation. CHURCH TIMES

□ The parson of a village where a friend of mine lives was perturbed at the persistent shortage of rain. Cattle and roots were suffering; the outlook was gloomy. He decided to pray for rain at morning service the next Sunday.

Then a troublesome thought struck him. 'No,' he told my friend, 'not next Sunday; I shall put it off till the Sunday after. I'M NOT GOING TO DO ANYTHING TO SPOIL THE TEST MATCH.' SUNDAY TIMES

□ King George of Greece was once bowled first ball in a cricket match at his English private school.

He never forgot the incident.

It helped him, he said, to face the poverty-stricken years of his exile with more courage than he might otherwise have shown.

It enabled him, he told friends, to treat the misfortune of his expulsion from Greece as a stepping-stone to ultimate triumph. SUNDAY REFEREE

□ Then came tragedy worse than anything devised by Aeschylus or Strindberg. Hammond played Grimmett to Wall at mid-wicket, and made no offer to run. Walters did run; so, then, did Hammond. The ball was returned to Grimmett, and Hammond was run out. LIVERPOOL DAILY POST

□ No one in England will be peevish at the passing of the Ashes. We have been

'*The Dance of Death*'

□ Well, I have had a letter from a friend in a Colony, where he exercises some sort of jurisdiction over natives, telling me that he has discovered an alternative to prison, namely, sharp fielding-practice at cricket for an hour. DAILY MAIL

□ Watson's was a fine display of solid competence. When his wicket fell the siren of a great barge passing down the Severn gave off a mournful and prolonged sound as though bewailing the departure of a kindred spirit. DAILY MAIL

□ 'Had Hitler and Mussolini been cricketers I do not think we should have had all this trouble that is going on in Europe to-day.' *Sir Francis Lacey, for 25 years Secretary of the M.C.C., at the annual meeting of the Wiltshire County Cricket Club, reported in the* MANCHESTER GUARDIAN

□ The colours of Nationalist Spain are the same as those of the M.C.C., and the familiar red and yellow glimpsed between the clouds of exploding shells awoke very different memories – indolent hours at Lord's, M.C.C. flags drooping listlessly in the summer haze. *Mr Arnold Lunn in* UNIVERSE

□ When Frank Groves, of Talbot Terrace, Leeds, was summoned at Great Yarmouth Police Court today for failing to conform with a traffic sign, the managing director of his firm wrote to the Bench: 'May I respectfully ask you to remember what Yorkshire did for England in the last Test Match?' CAMBRIDGE DAILY NEWS

beaten by a much better team. Oddly enough, and to the permanent bewilderment of foreigners, that is an experience in which Englishmen still find a keen enjoyment. *Leader in the* EVENING NEWS

□ One of the original regulations of I. Zingari read, 'I. Z. batsmen and fieldsmen, being hit, are not entitled to rub.' That was the spirit. OBSERVER

□ The headmistress of Godolphin, Miss C. R. Ash, was of the opinion that the school certificate for girls was only valuable if taken in their stride. She said that one of her best cricketers went entirely off her bowling last summer because of examination worries. NEWS CHRONICLE

The English are keen sportsmen in other fields too

□ Colonel Sir Lancelot Rolleston, D.S.O, a well-known Nottinghamshire fox-hunter and a former master of hounds, says: 'If foxes, like women, had a vote, I think they would vote unanimously for the keeping up of fox-hunting. ... I have known a fox that was absolutely devoted to fox-hunting . . . after we had hunted him many seasons, I regret to say we killed him.' DAILY MAIL

□ The principle of vicarious suffering pervades history, some suffering and dying for the good of others. The mother for her sick child, the doctor in his laboratory, the missionary among the heathen, the soldier on the battlefield – these suffer and sometimes die that others may live and be happy and well. Is it not in accordance with this great principle that animals should play their part by sometimes suffering and dying to help in keeping Britons hardy, healthy and brave, in providing healthful recreation for so many, in providing the means of livelihood for many thousands? *The Rev. J. Price (Vicar of Talley) on blood sports, reported in the* WESTERN MAIL

□ Great pleasure is expressed in the garrison at the kindness of Gen. Franco in permitting the Royal Calpe Hunt of Gibraltar to resume hunting in the neighbouring Spanish territory.

The Seville daily newspaper, ABC, referred to sport as being a necessity to Britons, especially hunting. The newspaper mentioned the fact that the King is patron of the hunt, and it expressed the hope that the British would be more polite to the Nationalists and, in view of the concession, not describe them as insurgents. DAILY TELEGRAPH

☐ 'I think,' said Colonel Lowther, 'that if we could get the dictators to come out with the Pytchley Hounds their attitudes towards life might change considerably, They would get a better idea of the meaning of real friendship.' NORTHAMPTON CHRONICLE AND ECHO

☐ The end came at the fourth, where Walsh cut his second shot into the famous Pow Burn. Dunlop would have shared the same fate, but by great good fortune, his shot struck a spectator and rebounded on to the green. DAILY TELEGRAPH

☐ It was revealed to-day that G. L. Rampling, who won the quarter mile for England in the British Empire Games in 48 seconds, actually ran a greater distance. . . . For the purposes of the record, the track at the White City, London, has been surveyed, and a certificate has been given stating that Rampling actually ran 440 yards three inches. This, of course, makes Rampling's feat all the more meritorious. YORKSHIRE EVENING POST

☐ The Bible is the inspiration of Louis. He always reads it before entering the ring, and then, according to one of his seconds: 'All fortified and everything, he just wades in and knocks the other guy's block off.' DAILY EXPRESS

☐ Perry to remain an amateur if he can make £20,000. DAILY TELEGRAPH

☐ There is something specially clean and wholesome about boating men of which one is not so conscious among other athletes. SUNDAY TIMES

☐ Every Sunday the papers come out with the same story of 'rough charging'. I can just imagine the reception a Rugger player would get if he asked for a hacked shin to be sponged! I was crocked for life in a sportsman's game, and I'm proud of it. *Letter in the* DAILY EXPRESS

☐ For two hours the committee of a golf club in south-east England debated whether women players might be allowed to wear trousers on the links. Their decision was: 'Trousers may be worn by women golfers on the course, but must be taken off on entering the clubhouse.' DAILY MIRROR

☐ To create an anti-moral effect on enemy bombers, why not co-ordinate and attach all our gun shots (sportsmen and keepers) to the Observer Corps and arm them with a light weapon effective up to 2,000 to 3,000 feet against enemy bombers? Properly controlled they would provide a devastating menace to the low bomber. I can see many a week-end party assembling on good beats. *Letter from Air Commodore P. F. M. Fellowes in* THE TIMES

☐ Herr Walter Funk, the German Finance Minister, is not the same Walter Funk who fought Pat MacAllister at the Nottingham Victoria Baths. NOTTINGHAM EVENING NEWS

☐ Aston Villa's further progress towards promotion was an antidote to the European scares. BIRMINGHAM GAZETTE

They have a great respect for other forms of animal life

□ The suggestion that men under sentence of death should be substituted for animals in vivisection experiments was made by the Lord Mayor of Portsmouth (Alderman Sir Harold Pink) at the annual meeting today of the South Hampshire and Portsmouth branch of the RSPCA. Alderman Pink said he had never cared for any sport which entailed the destruction of or damage to animal life, and he thought it would be advantageous to include in school curriculums the ethics of kindness to animals. EVENING STANDARD

□ The Hon. Mrs John Barran is one of the famous Ruthven twins and a daughter of Lord Ruthven. Her dachshund, Snoutie, follows the prevailing fashion of single pearl earrings and choker collar, and manages to look most attractive in them. SKETCH

□ Everyone knows that the Okapi is a member of the giraffidae family, and that he has a head intermediate between the giraffe and the prehistoric samotherium of the Lower Pliocene of Europe. OBSERVER

□ In character the Irish Terrier is what may be defined as a 'perfect gentleman' and moreover one is thoroughly aware of his status. For instance, the one I owned would always differentiate between guests, in whom he displayed a courteous interest, and the servants, whom he treated with polite indifference. *J. Wentworth Day in the* EVENING STANDARD

□ Cannot the ban on the importation of parrots into England now be removed, thereby giving an opportunity for English exiles with their parrots to return to their homes for the Royal Jubilee? *Letter in the* DAILY MAIL

☐ A dalmatian dog named Pongo Murgatroyd is a collaborator in Miss Dodie Smith's new play, *Call It A Day*. So she told me yesterday at the Glove Theatre, where the play is in rehearsal. She did most of the work on it while walking about the country near her Essex cottage in Pongo Murgatroyd's inspiring company. 'If he barked approval I knew I was on the right track,' she said. *Report in the* NEWS CHRONICLE

☐ After taking counts in all sorts of places in and around London this summer, my wife and I came to the conclusion that London's bird population was about two-and-a-half million strong with about 1,558,993 house-sparrows, 230,036 wood-pigeons and 32,040 domestic or wild homing pigeons. These are London's three commonest birds. STAR

☐ A dog usually possesses those fine qualities in which human beings are sometimes deficient. If your dog were suddenly to know you as you are, and not as he thinks you are, could you look him in the face? *Letter in the* STAR

RESULT OF APPEALS:
East Islington Mothers' and Babies' Welfare Centre, Marchioness of Lansdowne £49. 10. 8
People's Dispensary for Animals of the Poor, Christopher Stone* £11,812.0.9
* Promise of a further £1000
RADIO TIMES

☐ I personally own a bull terrier, and would say here and now that I have far more in common with my dog and any horse than I have with 99¾ per cent of the people I meet. *Letter in the* DAILY EXPRESS

☐ Certainly the death of a gallant horse like old True Blue or Avenger is a matter to mourn as one mourns the death of a gallant friend killed in war. There is something surely amiss with the man to whom Aintree, with its splendid spectacle of British courage and endurance, does not bring a catch in the throat. May its shadow never grow less, for it is – England. *Letter in the* DAILY TELEGRAPH

☐ The Mayor said he was a great animal lover, and he detested people who were cruel to animals. 'It is bad enough with children, but when it comes to dumb animals it is terrible,' he said. DORSET COUNTY CHRONICLE

□ A special corner by dogs for dogs will be included in 'Calling All Dogs', which the BBC are putting on next Sunday in honour of 'Eve of Dog-Licence Day'. The view at Broadcasting House is that, although dogs do not normally display much interest in the loudspeaker, they will if special material is broadcast for them. NEWS CHRONICLE

2

The War. Almost at once Britain is vacating France, and fighting a rearguard action at Dunkirk. Gas-masks, air raids, A.R.P., Home Guard, food rationing. Winston Churchill, conveniently caricaturable as a British bulldog, is adopted as war leader. The Japanese bomb unprotected Pearl Harbor, the base of the American Pacific fleet, and America enters the war. In 1942 the tide of war turns against Hitler with reverses at Stalingrad and El Alamein. In 1943 the Allies invade Italy. A year later they land in Normandy and the great push to Berlin begins. The Second World War ends not with a whimper but a bang, as the Americans try out the first A-bombs on the Japanese.

☐ But the Germans who matter, those under forty years of age, have been brought up in the belief that Great Britain is their hereditary enemy. Nothing but a sound thrashing will convince them of that error. *Field-Marshal Lord Milne in the* EVENING STANDARD

☐ After God, the Empire was surely the greatest power for good in the world. When trouble began, he said, other nations clustered around it like chickens around a hen. The Empire had enemies, continued the Major, but he believed them to be all part of God's plan in using the British Empire as an instrument for bringing about a better world. BRECON AND RADNOR EXPRESS

☐ If the Germans are suffering from RAF retributory bombing, it is because they have brought it on themselves. 'As ye sow so shall ye reap', and because the British race is the appointed instrument of Divine retribution. *Correspondent in the* GLASGOW HERALD

☐ 'It can confidently be stated,' Brig. General Lord Croft says in a foreword, 'that no single territory of the Empire fell to us as a result of premeditated aggression.' OBSERVER

☐ It will be noticed that the British Empire is particularly poorly off with regard to commercial sulphur deposits, which means that it is entirely dependent on foreign supplies, coming chiefly from the U.S.A. and Italy. It might be suggested that, following the successful outcome of hostilities with Italy, the British Government should demand the cession of Sicily as spoils of war and that this island should be incorporated in the Empire as a British Colony. MINING MAGAZINE

STORY OF THE BAYONET
A Weapon That Reveals National Character
EDINBURGH EVENING DISPATCH

□ Advocates of the much belauded decimal system have not noticed one of its drawbacks. In England, every clerk and shopman every man in a railway ticket office can do any amount of arithmetic sums in his head and get the answer right. People of less civilized lands cannot; they cannot do the sums, even on paper. *Letter in the* SUNDAY TIMES

□ 'T.W.B.' says that since the Russians have proved themselves to be such valiant fighters they should be asked to join the British Commonwealth of Nations as a token of our admiration. EDINBURGH EVENING NEWS

□ Great Britain has been responsible for nearly every major invention which has proved of benefit to the world. *A. M. Low in the* DAILY SKETCH

□ 'It is very un-English to bite people, and I would like you to impress that on these men,' said Mr J. H. Campbell, K.C., at Belfast Custody Court to-day to the captain of a Dutch ship who was acting as interpreter for three of his crew who were charged with disorderly behaviour at a dance hall in the York Street area last night.

The captain replied: 'It is very un-Dutch, too, your Worship.' BELFAST TELEGRAPH

□ Saying he was in favour of Rome being bombed, Councillor R. Richards, who was yesterday installed as President of the Eastbourne Chamber of Commerce, told the members that Eastbourne people considered Eastbourne was as beautiful as Rome. He had been in several Italian towns, and he considered that they had got nothing compared with this country. SUSSEX DAILY NEWS

□ It is, I think, the refusal to let Hitler or anybody else interfere with the good old British custom of afternoon tea, which has kept our country undefeated when others had capitulated. TIMES OF MALTA

□ He tried to look like an Englishman by smoking a pipe and playing golf at the Wimbledon Park Club.

But he showed his Prussianism occasionally by talking roughly to his wife when she made an error at bridge. SUNDAY DESPATCH

□ Sir Harold Mackintosh, Chairman of the National Savings Committee, speaking at a luncheon given yesterday by the London Central Board of the Licensed Trade, said there were rumours that the Government were borrowing so much that they would never be able to pay it back. 'No British Government has ever broken faith or done a dirty trick, or ever will.' YORKSHIRE POST

□ Miss Irene Ward, M.P., at Gateshead brotherhood yesterday said that what impressed her most on her recent trip was the Cathedral at Valetta, Malta. Of the several chapels within the building, the only ones that had been damaged were Italian and German. This, she thought, was the hand of providence, and from it we should learn a spiritual lesson. NEWCASTLE JOURNAL AND NORTH MAIL

□ I only knew one Japanese to give himself up. He came in and said he wanted to be an honorary member of the Honourable British Empire. We sent him off to a doctor as we suspected he was raving mad. *British Staff Officer, reported in the* EVENING STANDARD

☐ Liquidator offers quantity brooches and buttons symbolic of Britain and her Dominions; gilt and exquisitely enamelled Flag (encircling motto in blue enamel – 'What we have we hold'); 1,000 1s. each (50 per cent below cost). Wonderful commemorative gift to workpeople. *Advertisement in* THE TIMES

☐ The Palmer family of Camden Town and Cambridgeshire have failed in their great war-time ambition – to breed a red, white and blue Victory mouse before World War No. 2 came to an end. REYNOLDS NEWS

☐ . . . the other nations may tend to forget what they owe to English, the language of the free, and may even adopt something like Esperanto, which would give to all English-speaking people no more than equality with Czechs, Frenchmen and Chinese. *Letter in* HEADWAY

The leaders in war

□ Sir Neville Henderson, formerly British Ambassador in Berlin, speaking of Goering at Sleaford (Lincs) last night, said: 'He may be a blackguard, but not a dirty blackguard.' NEWS CHRONICLE

□ I saw the Duke and Duchess of Kent enjoying themselves immensely in the informal atmosphere of Mayfair's newest entertainment.

The ballroom was rigged up to resemble a dug-out behind the lines. There were sandbags round the walls instead of armchairs and couches, and the place was lit by candles.

The Duke confessed his surprise that so much realism could be achieved. DAILY SKETCH

□ Some people consider that were Malcolm MacDonald at the Bar he could if he so wished reach the office of Lord Chancellor.

How many know that the Colonial Secretary can walk on his hands and sing at the same time? ABERDEEN EVENING EXPRESS

□ Now, mention Europe to Anthony Eden, and a look of polite but quite genuine lack of interest comes into his eyes. SUNDAY TIMES

□ At Middlesbrough Police Court yesterday, a solicitor, asking for excuse from attendance of a client, said: 'In the first place he is a man of not very bright intellect. Secondly, he is employed on important Government work.' NEWCASTLE JOURNAL

□ Parents who want their children to grow up into good patriots are concerned over a recent circular issued by the Board of Education which says a teacher is at liberty to hold any political view he likes. DAILY SKETCH

☐ The most pathetic thing about Adolf Hitler was his passionate desire to be approved of by English gentlemen. DAILY TELEGRAPH

☐ The Duke of Hamilton . . . succeeded to the title last year, when his father died at the age of 78 . . . he is the only Peer who has broken his nose five times. DAILY HERALD

☐ It is conceivable that some devout element in Hess's character has gradually asserted itself, opening his eyes to the fundamental wickedness of the Nazi ambitions with which he has been so long associated. Such cases of swift conversion are not rare in history. Buddha turned from a life of royal luxury to found a great religion, St Francis d'Assisi was a loose-living reveller until he suddenly became one of the most saintly figures of all time. *G. Ward Price in the* DAILY MAIL

☐ 'A feeling spread abroad in some quarters that senior officers are a lot of old blimps is not shared by the War Office,' he declared. *Financial Secretary of the War Office*. DAILY MAIL

☐ A big effort to improve the intellectual standard of Conservative M.P.s is behind the Party Chief's move to make character and ability, rather than wealth, the qualification for adopting Parliamentary candidates. EVENING STANDARD

☐ Mr Zitelli says that no one who can select a fine cigar with the unerring instinct of Winston Churchill 'can possibly be anything but a very great gentleman'. NEWS CHRONICLE

☐ Karl Marx lived in London, and, being sincerely averse to doing an honest day's work, wrote articles denouncing capitalism. . . . He lives now only in the minds of adolescent theorists, who imagine that men can be seduced from patriotism and love of country by a windy dream of a new world built on universal destruction. *Beverley Baxter, M.P., in the* EVENING CHRONICLE

☐ Dear Comrade,
   I like the Duke of Bedford's articles. He is so beautifully sane. Thinking of him in terms of music, he is a Tone Poem, the loveliest of all music: '*Andante con-expressione*'. How much is due to lucky birth and an easy life, I wonder. *Letter in the* WORD

☐ A piece of cake, half-eaten by King George of the Hellenes, was auctioned by Lady Crosfield on the occasion of the presentation by the Greek King of a mobile canteen for the Y.M.C.A. to Princess Helena Victoria, president of the National Women's Auxiliary of the Y.M.C.A. in the grounds of St James's Palace. *Caption to a photograph in the* TATLER

Blimps? Blimps? we see no Blimps

□ A north-east of Scotland farmer who received a letter from a Government department instructing him to go on with his ploughing as he had not ploughed his whole quota, replied that his staff was depleted and that the lambing season had come upon him so that ploughing would have to be suspended for a short period.

He has received a reply instructing him to postpone the lambing season for a month. REYNOLDS NEWS

□ After his adoption, Capt. Mott-Radclyffe said that although he went to school at Eton with Douglas-Home, it would be a fight with the gloves off, as, in his opinion, independent candidates today were little better than Fifth Columnists. REYNOLDS NEWS

□ We want more autocrats. I am an autocrat, because by birth, breeding, and intelligence I am fitted to lead. *Mr Austin Hopkinson, M.P.* DAILY MAIL

□ 'The problem of India,' he told me, 'centres round two simple facts: first – the average Indian's expectation of life is twenty-three years, as distinct from fifty-five years in Britain; second – the average income per head in India works out at £7 per annum.'

His statistics prompted a disturbing query: To people with an average life-expectation of twenty-three years, what is the good of promises for the future? EVERYWOMAN

□ Lord Faringdon, speaking in the Indian debate in the Lords to-day, addressed the House as 'My dears'. When laughter had subsided he corrected himself to 'My Lords'. EVENING STANDARD

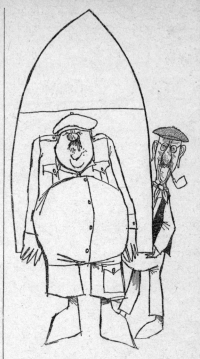

Cyril, he wants us to jump again

□ There is not enough discipline in the war factories. In my factory, when I tell the works to jump, they jump, or jump out. DAILY TELEGRAPH

□ His long legs dangling from the table, Sir John said; 'In these times we must make every sacrifice possible. But if a company director sees a loophole in the income tax laws he should make as much money as he can for his shareholders and himself.' *Interview with Sir J. Ramsden, Bt., in the* DAILY EXPRESS

□ The old school tie is as democratic an institution as the colours of the M.C.C. *Marquis of Exeter, reported in the* NEWS CHRONICLE

□ London is a town of nice surprises and at any moment you may run into the Queen doing some shopping, or see a swan fly over. NURSERY WORLD

□ Lady Montgomery, mother of General Montgomery, at Brixton yesterday, said that the last time her son was in London he went to get his hair cut. When it was finished there was a rush by customers and staff to collect the clippings. NEWS CHRONICLE

□ Mr Churchill says: 'We shall be envied by future generations our privilege of living in such stirring times.' If his message had been addressed solely to chiropodists, it would have been equally true. JOURNAL of the *Chelsea Chiropodists' Association*

□ It is doubly regrettable that when Mr Pethick-Lawrence opened the debate on famine in India, in the House of Commons, not more than 35 members were present. Dr Goebbels would normally make the most of such a fact, without disclosing the circumstance that it was lunch time. BOLTON EVENING NEWS

□ Sir,
Your reporting arouses my constant admiration, but I fear that I must have spoken indistinctly at the India Famine meeting yesterday. I am made to attribute to John Morley a statement that we had brought up the Indians 'on a diet of venom'; actually I said 'on Mill and Bentham'. *Letter to Editor of the* BIRMINGHAM POST

□ Viscount Selborne (Minister of Economic Warfare) replied that the term 'starving children' as applied to countries in Europe other than Greece in 1941, Poland and occupied Russia was entirely misleading. 'There is hunger, privation, malnutrition and distress, but nothing that can be called starvation.' THE SCOTSMAN

□ The Fleming Committee seek to throw open our Public Schools to all comers. Can anyone inform me what they seek to gain by this? I expect every woman would like a diamond necklace – but what would be its value if every woman possessed one. *Letter in the* DAILY SKETCH

□ The fifth Earl – was one of the old-fashioned earls – old-fashioned in the best sense. When he died last April, in his 79th year, he had 28 servants. DAILY MAIL

□ Sir Patrick Hannon is a Birmingham M.P. and his chairmanships and directorships run like a river through British industry. A great Empire figure, a good Catholic, a staunch friend, a tough Tory and a wise man. It is entirely right that he should own Magna Charta Island, where freedom was given its greatest charter. RECORDER

□ With regard to the post-war period, Lady Montgomery thinks it will be a much more difficult time for most of us than during the war years. One problem she could see was the finding of girls willing to enter domestic service after having been employed for so long in the Services, in the munitions, etc. LISBURN STANDARD

□ By the way, the Duchess of Kent unconsciously created much uneasiness by wishing to go down that coalmine in Durham. There is, I am told, a rule that the directors never go down the mines, and even for Royalty none of those present on the surface would descend. LIVERPOOL ECHO

☐ Sitting down to choose ribbons for the new campaign stars and medals announced by the Government yesterday, the King wanted to know the precise colour of the earth in a certain part of the bomb-fields. So some mud was scraped off the Field-Marshal Montgomery's car and sent to the King in a small box. DAILY EXPRESS

☐ In these democratic days when men rise from the humblest origins to the highest positions in the land, our old families are passing through a testing time. QUEEN

☐ Docking, Norfolk, Rural Council, have agreed to a petition by people living in Hell's Row, South Creake, to rename the district 'Churchill Estate'. EVENING STANDARD

☐ Six Labour Aldermen and Councillors of Altrincham, Cheshire, last night expressed disapproval that permission had been given to Sir Edward Grigg, eleven years M.P. for Altrincham, to take the title Lord Altrincham. ... The Mayor ... put the matter to the Sewage Disposal Committee, who granted Sir Edward's request by five votes to three. DAILY MAIL

☐ Consider, for instance, what the war speeches of Mr Churchill would sound like if, by some trick of fortune, they came to be read as the First Lesson in the churches of the distant future. Even their finest passages would echo round the nave with the same impressive unintelligibility as we associate with the oracles of Amos in our churches to-day. RADIO TIMES

☐ The Duke of Devonshire was elected president of the Society of Yorkshiremen in London yesterday, in succession to the Duke of Norfolk. NEWCASTLE JOURNAL AND NORTH MAIL

And the people keep a stiff upper lip

☐ My husband is a jolly good sort, one of those very hearty men. He wears plus-fours, smokes a long pipe, and talks about nothing but beer and Rugby football. My nerves won't stand much more of it. *A wife at Tottenham Police Court.* DAILY MAIL

☐ West End solicitors, who before the war netted five-figure incomes from divorce cases, have been heavily hit by the black-out. In the winter months, at any rate, private inquiry agents are helpless. Adultery cannot be proved because identification is impossible in the pitch dark. REYNOLDS NEWS

☐ You can always judge the prosperity of a city or country by the number of its millionaires. The more millionaires, the more prosperity. *Charles Graves in the* DAILY MAIL

☐ The discontinuance of first-class on the Underground is only one of several jolts to the social code which the war is giving us. Not that it matters: we can all afford to be a little more democratic for a few months, just as we change our clocks every year in the same case. *'Observator' in the* OBSERVER

☐ The moment Mr Stanley uttered the words 'unmarried wife' a quiver of excitement ran through the House. DAILY MAIL

☐ I protest against the lowering of moral tone in Glasgow and elsewhere during the last months. Theatres are permitting more risqué jokes. London shows have gone naked. Evenings in Edinburgh I see girls smoking shamelessly in trams. *Letter in the* DAILY EXPRESS

□ Membership is strictly limited as to numbers, so there is no fear that it will ever be overcrowded, or that uncongenial spirits or persons of a low class will ever bring a jarring note into the Club. The Abbey Club meets the needs of those who hitherto have been deterred from joining a Naturist Club by the fear that they may find as fellow-members some humble employee, the butler, baker, broker or the insurance man. Not that there is anything snobbish about the club. NATURIST

□ Art improves on Nature again. In the Vic-Wells ballet, *The Wise Virgins*, the audience thought they were seeing nudes. Actually dancers wore skin-pink tights, painted to resemble human anatomy. EVENING STANDARD

□ Though park railings in Manchester are being removed for scrap, the park gates will be retained and locked as usual at nights to indicate that the parks are in theory closed. DAILY DESPATCH

□ A plainly discernible letter B on the reverse side of leaves of corn is regarded by people in the North of the Island as a good omen for a British victory in the war. This phenomenon last appeared, it is stated, in 1918, when the Allies won the war which had lasted from 1914. ISLE OF MAN TIMES

□ The collapse of France occasioned little real surprise to those acquainted with her social history in the past 20 years. Since 1920, France has been drinking heavily. ASHORE AND AFLOAT

□ I found the better-off people had many more difficulties than working-class women. They told me how difficult it was not to be able to phone and get what they wanted. *Lord Woolton reported in the* MANCHESTER GUARDIAN

□ I said unthinkingly that it seemed to taste like any other brown bread. Then she told me it was a sample of the new Government wholemeal loaf.

On second thoughts I found I was favourably impressed. The bread has quality. It would go excellently with a glass of Fonseca 1920. PETERBOROUGH DAILY TELEGRAPH

□ I suggest that speakers in 'Children's Hour' should not use the word 'Hello' when addressing the children. Country children now invariably greet their elders with this word, spoken in anything but a respectful tone. *Letter in the* RADIO TIMES

□ Four-room bungalows costing about £130 each are to be proposed as temporary homes for bombed-out people. As these bungalows would not be a satisfactory form of housing in a post-war era, it will be suggested that they be utilized for old-age pensioners after the war. DAILY MIRROR

□ Sir Gerald thought it rather snobbish for a set to call themselves 'workers'. He thought 'masters and men' a nice way of putting it. DAILY HERALD

□ It is noted that the Vicar of St John's, Chelsea, has been writing recently in his Parish Magazine that 'Women are to blame for the cigarette shortage', and the Reverend Gentleman comments, *inter alia*, that, 'It is a very severe indictment on the so-called women of our land, that men find a difficulty in procuring smokes at this time.' TOBACCONIST AND CONFECTIONER

□ The native black population is so unimportant that beyond mentioning them and pointing out to the children that their civilization is that of the Stone Age, and that it is impossible to raise them to ours, it is wise to ignore them. Children are inclined to think that the black people of Australia are as important as the black people of Africa. TEACHERS' WORLD

□ DEBROY SOMERS AND HIS BAND. Fifth Symphony (Abridged Version) Columbia DX 1028. One of Beethoven's liveliest works. A grand piece, with victory emphasized throughout. THE AIRSCREW

□ The BBC 'High Command' can see a double meaning where others can't. Take Geraldo's ditty, 'Why Don't We Do This More Often?' Jackie Hunter and Dorothy Carless used to sing, 'Why don't we do this more often, just as we're doing *tonight*?'

The BBC version for broadcasting now runs, 'Why don't we do this more often, just as we're doing TODAY?' DAILY MIRROR

□ Lavender water was ordered to be sprayed round a fire station prior to a visit by the Regional Commissioner, the Earl of Dudley. REYNOLDS NEWS

□ Mr Cresswell submitted that it had been decided in the High Court that to call a person a cow was not abusive because the cow was a clean animal. *Extract from a police court report in the* THAMES VALLEY TIMES

□ A glance at *The Times* shows that a lot of children are born every day. *British Industrial Plastics Ltd advertisement in* PUNCH

□ '7. It is particularly requested that students will not engage in conversation with those of the opposite sex either in the College building or in the neighbourhood. *Infringement of this rule may lead to suspension, and in cases of repetition to expulsion.* Members of the same family may arrange to meet each other in the Waiting Room at the end of the day or at the lunch hour.' *Extracts from Regulations, Pitman's College, Southampton Row*

□ The Brains Trust of the City of Leeds Women's Conservative Association, meeting yesterday in the Leeds and County Conservative Club, decided that girls ought not to be allowed to go to school in slacks as it made them conspicuous and arrested their physical development. YORKSHIRE POST

(*a*) Ballotine de jambon Valentinoise
(*b*) Assiette Froide et Salade
Authorized translation by the management
(*a*) Hot Spam
(*b*) Cold Spam
Menu of the Strand Palace Hotel, midday, 5 February 1943

□ A BBC official stated that there was no likelihood of a woman being appointed to his (Mr Alvar Lidell's) job. Pressed to say why, he replied, 'She might have to read bad news.' REYNOLDS NEWS

□ Finding himself in a third-class railway carriage after he had bought a first-class ticket, Charles Joseph Silvertop, a farmer, of Burford, Oxford, pulled the communication cord and stopped the train. He complained of the inefficiency of the railway staff in directing him to the third-class compartment. DAILY TELEGRAPH

□ Because it is considered 'not quite nice' for music-hall performers to show their braces or too wide an expanse of shirt on the stage, the Board of Trade are allowing them to obtain double-breasted suits, by special licence. EVENING NEWS

□ . . . Queen Charlotte's Hospital – one of the most famous in the country – expectant mothers would have to book up eleven months ahead! That, said Miss Dare, the Matron, is the present position. SUNDAY PICTORIAL

□ Dr T. H. Sanderson-Wells, Food Education Society Chairman, told in London yesterday of a perfectly balanced chemical meal, containing all the necessary vitamins, which was fed to a number of rats. They all died. DAILY MAIL

□ A woman who has become a mother should never come into public life. All mothers become, if not completely crackers, at least mentally unbalanced. *Answer to a question about women in Parliament, put to the Brains Trust*

□ The milk supplied to Lanarkshire schools was excellent. There may be an odd bottle with a beetle or snail in it, 'but that won't do you any harm'. GLASGOW EVENING NEWS

□ One thousand seven hundred girls have replied to the Mayor of Saffron Walden (Councillor Wilson) who recently appealed on behalf of a sailor who wanted girl pen friends 'with a view to matrimony'. NEWS CHRONICLE

□ They also asked for a woman expert representative on the Board's advisory corset panel, which is at present composed entirely of men. NEWS CHRONICLE

□ Governors of Fishguard (Pembs) County School are divided on the question of bare-legged teachers.

Said one governor (a man): 'Pupils have to wear stockings, but teachers go with bare legs. There can be no discipline.' SUNDAY EXPRESS

□ Sir,

Some of my older friends in Newmarket have told me of the exploits of the late Captain Machell, who when well in the fifties would take a flying leap and jump on the mantelpiece and stand there. Is there something sprightly in the East Anglian air? *Letter in* THE TIMES

□ 'We should make education of boys and girls quite different from the age of fourteen. Girls should be trained in more feminine occupations and boys should be given some form of military training. We should initiate the true line of evolution, like cows and bulls.' DAILY MIRROR

□ I am 16 years of age and was brought up in an orphanage. I was flogged over a thousand times and never found cause to regret it. As a child I hated the people who performed on me, but I am able to say now that they did me a great kindness. *Letter in the* NEWS CHRONICLE

□ When the *Telegraph and Argus* tried to interview Alderman H. Hudson, chairman of the Holidays-at-Home Committee, this morning, they were informed that he had gone away for his holidays and was not likely to be back in Bradford for at least ten days. BRADFORD TELEGRAPH AND ARGUS

□ The Merchant Navy have faced death for you . . . you are asked to dance for them at St Botolph's Hall. *Advertisement in the* LINCOLNSHIRE ECHO

☐ To my astonishment I find I am going to have a baby. I am just 18, and my boy friend and I have never done anything but kiss and hold hands. Can you tell me how it happened? WOMAN'S OWN

☐ Help to win the Peace by selling your vacant, blitzed property to a speculator, who will pay cash. *Advertisement in the* PORTSMOUTH EVENING NEWS

☐ There are not many turkeys to trouble the Post Office this year, but any amount of rabbits. The most tiresome repacking job of the season, said one of the workers, was a stew sent from London to Cambridge for a dog's dinner and wrapped in six newspapers. She poured off the gravy and gave it another chance. *Report in the* MANCHESTER GUARDIAN

☐ Tinned salmon is to have new labels. In the past the various species of salmon were graded one, two and three.

Because the Ministry of Food thought that this form of grading misled the public into thinking that these are three different qualities of fish, the three species will now be known as group one, group two, and group three. *Report in the* NEWS OF THE WORLD

☐ Because it has been ascertained that her brother is a conscientious objector, Miss Elsie Sutton, 18-year-old typist at a Potteries factory, of Scragg Street, Packmoor, Stoke-on-Trent, has been refused the role of the 'Spirit of Freedom' in a Burslem factory pageant, for which she was chosen a fortnight ago. DAILY MAIL

☐ Six Barrow-in-Furness gravediggers have begun an unofficial strike for higher wages because, in the words of one of them, they were being 'worked to death' in the cemetery. MANCHESTER GUARDIAN

☐ A cook is a male or female worker of 21 years of age or over wholly or mainly engaged in the preparing and cooking of food requiring the mixing of two or more ingredients with, or without, assistance. *Industrial and Staff Canteen Undertakings Wages Board*

☐ Men have always smoked. With women it is just a habit. *Letter in the* BRADFORD TELEGRAPH AND ARGUS

☐ She was a firm believer in 'votes for women', anti-vaccination, and Count Mattei's electro-homoeopathic globules. *From an obituary notice in* THE TIMES

☐ A headmistress wrote to the North Eastern District Education Committee yesterday saying she made girls scrub their tongues because 'She had never heard such an epidemic of bad language.'

In a report to the Committee it was alleged that carbolic soap was used, and one father complained that his daughter's mouth was so sore that she could not eat.

The Committee left the matter with the school managers. NEWS CHRONICLE

Women at war

□ Yes, we are assuredly returning to black, but it will be black with the most original touches. For example, one little tailor-made suit had five yellow medals dangling from the waist on gilt chains. These were inscribed 'Tittle-tattle lost the battle' – a timely warning, as well as an effective decoration. *Woman's Page*, GLASGOW BULLETIN

□ Sir James Marchant, one of the Salvage chiefs, in a speech in London today, gave as an example of wanton extravagance the case of a woman who confessed before the Birthrate Commission that she had 90 nightgowns, each scented with a different perfume to please her husband. LIVERPOOL ECHO

□ The coiffure seen in the accompanying picture was designed to represent the 'warring nations'. The bold upward sweep on the side of the head typified Britain's sturdy resistance and recovery; on the opposite side a long falling roll illustrated German decline. The United States was symbolized in the design, and curls represented the smaller Allied nations. DERBY EVENING TELEGRAPH

□ For the corset position was today described to me by the trade as 'more tragically dreadful than it has ever been'. EVENING STANDARD

□ Belsen and Buchenwald have put a stop to the too-thin woman age, to the cult of under-nourishment. VOGUE

□ Do your ears fan out? Try pasting them back with theatrical spirit gum. Press the ear flat, after applying the gum – until dry. VOGUE

The war effort is total

□ An old lady living at Wimbledon has sent a hot water bottle to the Lord Lieutenant of Surrey's Comforts Fund, with instructions that it should be sent to Stalin. YORKSHIRE EVENING POST

□ Flight Lieutenant Raikes (Cons., S.E. Essex) declared that, following a speech by the Prime Minister, saying we would defend our airfields even if we had only pikes, at several RAF stations pikes were at once ordered. DAILY EXPRESS

□ Home Guard men on the invasion coastline of Lincolnshire want to form a company of archers. Yesterday they showed their skill with bow and arrow to a general inspecting armoury. The general was impressed. Lieutenant Davey said to an *Express* reporter: 'On a moonlight night a skilled archer could kill silently from a distance.' DAILY EXPRESS

□ SOUTHERN MALAYAN TIN
DREDGING
Accounts Disclose Sound Position
Estate in Enemy Hands
THE TIMES

□ Now that soap is in short supply, is it not every true patriot's duty to grow a beard and moustache. He will save not only soap, but much valuable time. DAILY TELEGRAPH

□ Sir Noel Curtis-Bennett said at Westminster: 'If we apply the Fundamental principles of golf to our relations with our Allies we cannot go far wrong.' SUNDAY GRAPHIC

□ Now that admission to places of entertainment in Oxford is not conditional on the carrying of a gas mask, I can reveal (writes a country correspondent) the deception practised by some patrons.

63

In many cases people, especially those from the country, used their gas masks to carry some of the articles they had collected in their shopping expeditions. OXFORD MAIL

□ As waste paper is so urgently needed, would it not be wise to make use of the thousands, or hundred of thousands, of copies of books stored in the British Museum? What better use could be made of them than making them serve the country? *Letter in a daily paper*

□ The greatest Army manoeuvres ever held in Britain have just ended with the battle of Bedfordshire. Fighting for nearly a week led to the complete defeat of an enormous force which was supposed to have invaded England from the sea. Realism reached such a pitch during the operations that no fewer than 19 officers and men were killed in accidents. The total number of deaths may prove to be even higher. DAILY TELEGRAPH

□ I was watching a squad of soldiers drilling on the barrack square and was surprised to see one of them marching with two rifles (at the short trail). Upon asking the reason for this, I was informed by a sergeant that the owner of the second rifle was ill, but his rifle had to go on parade just the same as usual. *Letter in the* NEWS CHRONICLE

□ 'Raids have become almost a commonplace with us,' says Mr Peddie. 'No one thinks of talking about one the morning after – *unless they have had a direct hit.*' DAILY MAIL

□ Men are moved by ideals, as wartime propaganda proved. They will die to make a world safe for democracy even twice in a lifetime. NEW STATESMAN

□ 'It was quite a thrilling moment when the U-boat sank,' he said, 'but such is the sang-froid of the modern British seaman that there was no burst of cheering, only a little polite hand-clapping from the gun crews.' REYNOLDS NEWS

□ There is a school for jungle warfare in India where the only textbook used is a thin volume of Kipling's poems. An instructor at the school maintains that Kipling has the complete answer to almost every problem likely to be encountered during jungle operations.
'And,' he adds, 'a couplet on forays from Kipling can always be remembered, which is more than can be said for a military manual.' THE TIMES

□ The genteel village spinster patrolling in the dark, perhaps somewhat fearfully, may be almost a figure of fun, but the thought of her must irritate our would-be invader as the thought of the Kentish hedgerows irritated Napoleon. EVENING NEWS

□ Hastings has introduced a cuckoo-like sound in place of the air-raid siren. SUNDAY EXPRESS

□ But the strangest job of all is done by the A.T.S. – keeping moths out of 7,000 bearskin caps of the Brigade of Guards. SUNDAY EXPRESS

□ WE STILL OWE IT TO THE FEW THAT THERE BE MANY MORE
This space kindly given by H. C. Patrick Ltd, Monumental Masons, Funeral Directors, East Street, Farnham. *Advertisement from the* FARNHAM HERALD

□ The nice problems that arise amongst naval personnel of different ranks now that both sexes are in the Senior Service were exemplified by a recent incident in a Glasgow tea-room. Two pretty Wren ratings, seeing no available seats except at a table where a naval officer was sitting, took them.

The naval officer ignored them, but sent for the manageress, and asked her to accommodate the Wrens elsewhere. Discipline must be maintained, and nobody knows how his sense of duty struggled with his inclinations. GLASGOW HERALD

☐ The nephew of an Ealing councillor lost a pocket-book containing over £9 in Treasury notes. It was found in a neighbouring suburb by a German, who took it to the nearest police station, where he was thanked, asked his name and detained for internment. WEST MIDDLESEX GAZETTE

☐ 'I found that by removing the glass the mask fitted me much better and was much more comfortable,' said a Windsor woman reprimanded by a warden for taking out the eyepieces from her gas mask. EVENING NEWS

☐ My husband has just returned from a compulsory Home Guard parade. This consisted of an address by his battalion commander on 'The Early History of India from 1513–1717'. *Letter in the* PICTURE POST

☐ By the way, that Home Guard officer with the D.S.O. and bar whose message to the civilians I printed here last week has now inaugurated a mess dinner. The idea is to get the fellows together, and it is doing a lot of good. They wear denim uniform over a boiled shirt and a butterfly collar. *Charles Graves in* THE DAILY MAIL

☐ His Majesty's Motor Torpedo Boats, fifty-mile-an-hour speedboats, armed with eight Lewis guns and two torpedo tubes, are the Mosquitoes of the Royal Navy. The first eighteen of one class of these deadly craft were numbered 1 to 19. No Number Thirteen! It's just a detail, but a certain pointer to the care for detail that gives the Royal Navy its supremacy on the seas. *Trade advertisement in* THE TIMES

☐ It is impossible to forecast with definite accuracy the future course of the war – now started on its third year – for the good and sufficient reason that its course will be dictated by the successes and victories of one side or the other. *Sir Hubert Gough in the* GLASGOW DAILY RECORD

☐ Dive-bombers, it would appear from evidence I have been able to collect from various sources, have no frightening effect on Russian troops, who manage to deal faithfully with them in that unconcerned, rather genial manner with which they perform all tasks. NEWS CHRONICLE

☐ And Patrick's Irish blue eyes flash red, until the colours merge like the blue and red bars of his Military Medal ribbon. SOUTHPORT GUARDIAN

☐ Mrs Bunce went to make bombs; small, pretty bombs, turned and shaped by her gentle, domesticated hands. DAILY EXPRESS

☐ Pots, chamber plain
Pots, chamber, with admiralty monogram in blue, for hospital use
Pots, chamber, fluted, with royal cypher in gold, for Flag Officers only.
Pots, chamber, round, rubber, lunatic.
From Admiralty Stores List

□ Saluting, so far from being a tribulation, is a pleasure, and, indeed, when in an exuberant mood I have frequently crossed the road simply to get near enough to a general to salute him. *Letter in the* DAILY TELEGRAPH

□ Experienced general clerk (female) wanted for recording and other work in connexion with the personnel of the Fire Guard Organization; should be able to type and must be capable of interpreting Government orders and instructions. WATFORD OBSERVER

□ The sale of bedding was interrupted for a moment by the somewhat previous announcement that the German Air Force had surrendered, and, after brief but quite credulous applause, feather beds were sold for 10s., mattresses with pillows and bolsters from £3 5s. to £5, a cannon for 25s. and a pair of stuffed pheasants in a case for 5s. WORKSOP GUARDIAN

□ The extermination of the German nation would not be the solution of the problem. If eighty million spirits (many undeveloped) were suddenly hurled into the Beyond it would create a problem that baffles the imagination. *Letter in the* MIDDLESEX COUNTY TIMES

□ In part of Southern England, where mixed heavy A.A. batteries are fighting the incoming flying bombs 24 hours a day, there is another battle raging. It is being fought by people who just don't like noise – whether it be flying bombs or Ack-Ack guns. So far, more than a dozen have briefed solicitors, who are requesting that the military authorities be asked to move the gunners. NEWS CHRONICLE

□ Accounts of humorous incidents, as well as others unspeakably grim, are circulated in Athens. In 'No-Man's-Land' a resident with only the slightest knowledge of English was halted by a British tank. He was asked for his name and address, which he willingly gave.

Immediately afterwards the tank plopped three shells into the unfortunate man's house. A typical Athenian, the man saw the joke, laughing heartily when the coincidence was later explained by the tank crew. *Richard Cappell in the* DAILY TELEGRAPH

□ Social Crusade Special Open-Air Services in the parks and recreation grounds of Leeds during the summer of 1945, at which D. B. Foster hopes to speak on the big issues before the world . . . should the war in Germany and Japan come to an end during the above period, the last 10 minutes of each meeting afterwards will be devoted to explaining the supreme evil of smoking. *Notice in the* SOCIAL CRUSADER

In time of war men look to their God

☐ A black poodle, owned by the Vicar of Bodmin, was adjudged to be most like its owner from a motley array of dogs and owners who paraded at the comic dog show held in connexion with the fête to raise funds for the Bodmin Sub-depot of the Central Hospital Supply Service yesterday. NEWSPAPER EXPRESS

☐ St Paul's Cathedral badly damaged, and now the Middle Temple. I say destroy Cologne Cathedral; bomb St Peter's, Rome; let the Fleet bombard Genoa and destroy men, women and children, and marble palaces. *Letter from Rev. S. F. Cottam in the* OXFORD MAIL

☐ Rev. Jimmy Haddow, Glasgow's conjuring minister, has died. He found he could do conjuring tricks when he was twelve years of age and it was this which led him to take up the Ministry. SUNDAY PRESS

□ Boy and girl friendships should not be tolerated by Catholic parents; they not only rob young girls of that modesty and that reserve which is the charm of their sex and age but they are positively dangerous. To shrink from corporal punishment in these circumstances is not a sign of love; rather it is a sign of weakness and blindness to the child's earthly and eternal welfare. *Bishop of Salford, quoted in the* MANCHESTER GUARDIAN

□ The Chairman of the Finance Committee, who recommended Leach's dismissal, said there were no conscientious objectors allowed in the Old Testament, and they should not be allowed in these days. DAILY HERALD

□ After a silver wafer box worth £4 had been stolen from Runwell, Essex, parish church – one of several recent thefts – the rector posted this notice on the church door:

'The thief may be quite sure that unless he (or she) restores it a blight will rest upon himself and his family. Christian experience has found this invariably to be true.' SUNDAY EXPRESS

□ A new edition of the Bible, specially written for 'the man-in-the-street' and illustrated with pictures of tanks, marching armies and aeroplanes, is to be published on 10 July. NEWS CHRONICLE

□ Are we not the instruments of Divine Retributive Justice, and must not our Cause therefore be secure? Shall not the Judge of all the earth do right? If He fails us in this issue His very character is suspect. *Prof. Maurice Ralton in the* CHURCH OF ENGLAND NEWSPAPER

□ Holy Trinity, Hoxton. Assistant Priest required. Title would be considered. Young and able-bodied, early riser, clean and tidy appearance. Pacifists, Communists, or men contemplating marriage need not apply. *Advertisement in the* CHURCH TIMES

□ God was not just a referee watching and controlling the game from aloof, but rather He was the centre forward of the home team, helping to shape its course, said the Bishop of Bradford (Dr A. W. F. Blunt) at a Youth Rally on Wednesday. BLACKBURN TIMES

□ Eight Brighton clergymen concealed from view will represent the Voice of God when the sixteenth century Spanish morality play *The Theatre Of the World* is produced in a Brighton Church next week. SOUTH WALES ECHO

□ Mrs Richards, daughter of the late Mr Justice Grantham, said that she was 'in favour of the birch' and believed it should be given to mean, despicable boys. If such boys could be given Christianity as well Britain would have a finer race.

'Christianity and beating should go together,' she declared. DAILY WORKER

□ The Dean of Ely said at Ely yesterday: 'The use of the birch is not to be deplored. All the best men in the country have been beaten, archbishops, bishops, and even deans. Without sensible correction they would not be the men they are to day.' MANCHESTER GUARDIAN

□ The chairman of the Methodist District deprecated the holding of harvest thanksgiving services in public houses, but he thought that good work might be done by dropping into a licensed house and talking to the men over a glass of lemonade. NEWS CHRONICLE

□ In evidence P. C. Thomas Roberts said defendant was a Jehovah's Witness, and when he stopped her and told her she would be reported for not having a red rear light, she looked up at the full moon, which was shining brightly that night, and said: 'You are ignoring God's gift from above.' CAMBRIAN NEWS

□ The first business of the day is Prayers. The Chaplain stands up, with the Speaker next to him. The Chaplain looks at the Members of Parliament, and then he prays for the country. *Lecture on 'Parliamentary procedure' by Sir Edward Campbell*

□ The Rector, who organizes weekly dances in the Public Hall for the Forces in the neighbourhood, said the title 'Doodle-bug dance' was meant to imply that the fun would be fast and furious and that the dance would 'go with a bang.' HERTS ADVERTISER

□ Mr Barclay says in his parish magazine: 'I know a "live church" in South London where a football service is held. The local football club members attend in their jerseys and miniature goal posts are erected over the pulpit. When the vicar has preached for ten minutes someone blows a whistle and shouts half-time.' DAILY MIRROR

□ Fourteen years ago Mrs B. took her own sick son to Lourdes. 'He was not cured,' she said, 'but our Lady of Lourdes did not forget him. He died suddenly on her Feast Day.' DORSET DAILY ECHO

□ The delegates [at an inter-church Conference called by the British Council of Churches] all agreed that the atom bomb was the voice of God. EVENING STANDARD

□ Will you kindly give your opinion whether doing crossword competitions is displeasing to God? – R.R.
I can well believe that such competitions are most entertaining and instructive, and certainly there is not the slightest reason, from the Christian point of view, why you should not indulge in what is, surely a perfectly innocent pastime, when no money transactions are involved. CHRISTIAN HERALD

□ When the case was resumed after lunch Mr Justice Lawrence said to Miss Bennett: 'Do you understand the English language. A *subpoena* commands you to attend the court.' DAILY HERALD

□ When Evan Evans, aged 17, was found guilty of stealing a bicycle by the Cardiff magistrates today it was stated that he had been to sea recently and after his ship was torpedoed he and 40 other survivors were afloat in an open boat for 14 days and nights before being rescued. 'I should have thought torpedoing would have put something better into you,' said Mr J. Ash Thompson, chairman. SOUTH WALES ECHO

□ When the nature of an oath was being explained to a 10-year-old boy at Bletchley Police Court on Thursday, the Chairman asked him: 'Whom do you offend against if you tell a lie?'
The boy: The Rector.
The chairman: Someone above the Rector; who is it?
The boy: Hitler!
The lad's evidence was not taken on oath. LEIGHTON BUZZARD OBSERVER

☐ Mr Marriott's views will be heartily endorsed by the Chairman of the Northampton Juvenile Court (Mr G. W. Beattie) who has repeatedly advocated whipping, and recently told one young scapegrace: 'I should like to give you a good thrashing myself, even although it would hurt me more than it would you', whereupon the impudent young urchin merely assumed a cynical smile. NORTHAMPTON INDEPENDENT

☐ 'Approved schools rank almost as high as some of the best public schools,' the Magistrate at North London juvenile court told a boy of 15, who said he would rather go to prison than return to an approved school. The lad was sent back to an approved school. DAILY TELEGRAPH

☐ An 89-year-old woman, Ellen Haworth, of Salesbury, near Blackburn, was stated at Blackburn inquest yesterday to have never had a bath. The coroner said that her death of senility was accelerated by gross neglect. MANCHESTER GUARDIAN

☐ When a boy of 9½ years was being examined in an action for damages at Newry Quarter Sessions yesterday Judge Begley asked if he knew what would happen to him if he did not tell the truth. 'I'll be sent to hell,' said the boy, and his Honour replied: 'That is true Christianity.' NORTHERN WHIG AND BELFAST POST

☐ The flat was formerly occupied by the Duchess of Windsor before her marriage, and is the most expensive flat the police have ever visited in connexion with a murder mystery. DAILY MIRROR

☐ Frederick Charles Peel, police superintendent of the Arundel Division, appeared at Littlehampton today on a summons taken out by himself for having permitted an unobscured light to show from one of his windows at the divisional headquarters. DAILY HERALD

☐ As secretary of the British Snail-Watching Society I must protest against Frances Pitt's light-hearted nature story about the way of a thrush with a snail. Such matters must be recorded objectively in natural history books but the snail's unpleasant fate should not be treated semi-humorously to make a Roman or any other kind of holiday. *Letter in the* SUNDAY GRAPHIC

'*Stand still, you bastard*'

□ My dog was loaned to the Ministry of Aircraft Production over two years ago. Since when, apart from a censored letter once a month from his keeper, I have never seen him. Surely now some of these dogs could be returned. *Letter in the* SUNDAY EXPRESS

□ Alleged to have killed and eaten a sheep he caught in his garden, a labourer received two months' imprisonment. The offence was revealed through a policeman noticing a lamb crying outside the house. NEWS CHRONICLE

□ A five-years-old Chertsey hen has laid four double-yolked eggs in a competition for the Red Cross. SUNDAY EXPRESS

□ The Admiral hasn't had news of his wife and five children since he was compelled to leave them behind in Bandoeng. He does not even know the fate of his pet monkey that used to shin up and down the trees in the grounds of his spacious Batavis residence. NEWS REVIEW

□ Dog for Sale, eats anything. Fond of Children. *Advertisement in the* HAYES NEWS

□ The Secretary of the National Canine Defence League protests against suggestions that dogs should no longer bear the owner's name and address because this information might be useful to enemy parachutists. He gives the following reasons why no parachutist is likely to receive help in this way: the animal would be too intelligent, or particular, to permit a Hun to examine him; the Hun would get bitten, and anyone who stopped to read dog collars would be advertising very clearly that he was up to mischief. THE TIMES

□ Sylvia Countess Poulett (60) described as independent, of London, was fined £5 at Harrogate yesterday for showing a light from her bedroom at an hotel. Police-Sergeant Haig said that when he interviewed Lady Poulett on 8 Sept. she explained that the light had been left on in her room so that her little dachshund could eat its supper. SUNDERLAND ECHO

Sport has a place in war

□ An amusing situation has arisen among well-known sportswomen who are now stationed at a WATS officers' training unit on the South Coast.

Miss Elizabeth Glascock, the squash player, is training the cricketers, Myrtle Maclagan and Kitty de Gex (Oxford), for whom she 'fagged' at the Royal School, Bath. NEWS CHRONICLE

□ A cricket Blue, by the way, was telling me the other day of his experiences on the beach at Dunkirk. He said that one of the things that impressed him was that it would have been possible to pick up two first-class 'Gentlemen *v.* Players' sides. DAILY TELEGRAPH

□ A ball moved by enemy action may be replaced as near as possible where it lay, or if lost or destroyed a ball may be dropped not nearer the hole without penalty. *New golf rule reported in daily paper.*

□ Can any reader tell me the correct way to carry a shot fox? In the conditions of today there is credit rather than obloquy in adding a 'red dog' to the game bag, and at least it should be carried off the field in triumph. But how? The hare and rabbit I can manage; the pheasant, too; but when I saw a keeper carrying a 'red dog' by grasping all four pads and allowing the head to hang backwards at one end and the brush to trail at the other, I felt there was something wrong. *Letter in the* BIRMINGHAM POST

□ Golfers, already assisting the war effort, are to help still further by playing on courses that have been shortened by ploughing. NEWS CHRONICLE

□ Loyal millions far beyond the reckoning are fervently hoping that His

Majesty the King will win the Oaks and the Derby with Sun Chariot and Big Game. The names of these horses are already known throughout the universe, but not as yet have they earned the right to fame eternal. STAR

□ The remarkable circumstances in which Edward Winter, a taxi proprietor, of Gresford, was alleged to have wasted motor fuel were related before the Wrexham County Magistrates yesterday. Complaints have been received by the police, who kept observation on the Wrexham golf links and saw the defendant driving his taxi along the fairway. Asked to explain, Winter replied that he had a 93-year-old player inside who was too weak to walk. MANCHESTER GUARDIAN

□ Portsmouth City Councillors donned their cricket flannels yesterday. It was not only a reminder of the happy days of peace when they regularly played the civic fathers of Southampton and Brighton, but also an indication of the turn of the tide in war. PORTSMOUTH EVENING NEWS

□ The Venerable E. R. Buckley, Archdeacon of Ipswich, writing in the St Edmundsbury and Ipswich Diocesan magazine to-day discussing whether cricket or football is the more 'spiritual' game, has decided in favour of cricket. EVENING STANDARD

□ . . . for without foxes there would be no foxhunting, and without foxhunting many would find it impossible to live through an English peace-time winter. HORSE AND HOUND

□ A major said: 'Only a few young bloods are fraternizing. What we want here are cricket bats, not frauleins.' DAILY EXPRESS

3

Post-war years. Demobilization, and the men who won the war return to elect not their heroic war-time leader, Churchill, but a Labour government headed by Clement Attlee. This is the beginning of nationalization as the State buys up coal and steel and civil aviation and the railways. At the same time, Britain gently loosens her grip on the British Empire, and notably surrenders India.

□ Our officers and men in Germany and Austria are doing a grand job in just being British. DAILY SKETCH

□ The 'Jacobites' in fact, are taking part in the preliminary shooting of the Technicolor film of 'Bonnie Prince Charlie'. . . . To ensure that no fires of latent anger be kindled in English hearts, Sir Michael Bruce, the historical adviser, has stated that the cruelties committed after Culloden are to be attributed to the German troops which fought under Cumberland. STAR

□ In *The Verdict of You All* there are really no holes to pick, it is an English murder, and does our country credit. *Back cover of a Penguin detective story*

□ It is not going too far to say that at least half of our soccer defeats abroad would be avoided if English – or equally unbiased – referees were in charge. STAR

□ Our people in the past have built empires, invented wonders, withstood blitzes and won wars on the good plain cooking of the Englishwoman. I am confident they will eventually win the peace on the same stuff. *Letter in the* NEWS CHRONICLE

□ King Leopold is indistinguishable from an Englishman of the finest type – so that it comes as a surprise when he breaks into fluent French. *Letter in the* EVENING STANDARD

□ Chief hangman Albert Pierrepoint met trouble only once in all the hundreds of executions he carried out, and that was with a spy. 'He was not an Englishman,' Pierrepoint said. DAILY HERALD

□ The English are a forgiving nation. They forgave Southern Irish, Italians, Bulgarians, Germans, Rumanians, Slavs. Is it not time that the Duke of Windsor and his wife were 'forgiven'. *Letter in the* EVENING STANDARD

The new leadership

☐ Mr Pritt (Hammersmith, N., Ind. Lab.) asked how the question of tea stocks was relevant to the debate.

The speaker said he did not hear what Mr Pritt said. He thought he was asking about the bread ration. (Laughter.)

Mr Pritt again asked how the question of tea stocks could be relevant to the order relating to soap.

The speaker. Cheese does not seem to have much to do with soap, but some cheese is rather like soap. (Loud laughter.) THE TIMES

☐ The fête was opened by Mrs O. L. Prior-Palmer, wife of Worthing's M.P. She told her audience: 'Many people are still apt to ask what the Conservatives want so much money for. Money is essential for propaganda. We shall never get the Socialists out of power by waiting for them to make mistakes.' WORTHING HERALD

☐ Declaring it open, Mr Churchill said: 'I earnestly hope that out of this war will come not only a just and wise settlement among the people of Europe and the world, but also that England will stand erect among nations and march ever forward along our gallant and glorious past.' SUNDAY TIMES

☐ His sympathy, understanding and regard for the Spanish people were surpassed only by his devotion to your company's interests. *Company Report in* THE TIMES

☐ Mr Ernest Bevin, the Foreign Secretary, speaking at the miners' rally at Morpeth, Northumberland, said he had never worked in a Cabinet which had shown a better team spirit. There were no jealousies, no quarrels, no anything. OBSERVER

☐ Perhaps one of the most insistent inquiries from overseas has been on where the Royal couple will live after their marriage. The fact that the Princess and her husband will probably have to share Buckingham Palace with their parents has done more than any amount of propaganda to convince the rest of the world that there is a housing shortage in Britain. WEEKLY TELEGRAPH

☐ 'The Conservatives do not believe it necessary, and, even if it were, we should oppose it,' he declared. *Mr Quintin Hogg, M.P., reported in the* OXFORD MAIL

☐ The Duke of Gloucester, by the way, is called Clapper in the family circle, on account of his habit of attracting the attention of servants or his children by clapping his hands. SUNDAY PICTORIAL

☐ Sir Ralph Glyn (Con., Abingdon) suggested that there might well be places such as Balmoral scattered throughout the Commonwealth which the Royal family could go to to mix with their subjects. NEWS CHRONICLE

☐ 'Everybody in the Empire should spend an hour or so with the King or Queen.' EVENING STANDARD

☐ Princess Elizabeth will not get the £4 free grant which the State makes to mothers on the birth of their babies, because Prince Philip has not paid enough contributions on his National Health Insurance card. PEOPLE

☐ The baby Prince is reported to be doing well, and to be a very healthy active boy, who behaves day and night as a Prince might be expected to do. NURSING MIRROR

☐ Princess Margaret seems on the way to becoming a House of Commons 'fan'. The Princess herself declared that the House gives her a chance of seeing human nature 'in the raw' such as she seldom has elsewhere. GLASGOW BULLETIN

☐ 'There is a simple answer to the atom bomb,' says dapper, quiet-voiced Brigadier A. M. Toye, V.C., M.C. 'It is that no weapon has ever been invented for which the answer doesn't exist.' ILLUSTRATED

☐ Official reports to the Colonial Office prove that Britain's use of forced labour in the colonies is extremely limited and mainly for the benefit of the natives themselves. NEWS CHRONICLE

☐ What lifted the audience of Tories to their feet was the sudden realization that this man believed the things the Tories always say. DAILY EXPRESS

☐ Tories as well as Socialists should question the wisdom of granting to the three-years-old Prince Charles an income of £10,000 a year. It is never good for a young boy to have too much money to spend. DAILY EXPRESS

☐ There is an ornament standing in Mrs Lena Atkinson's prefab . . . it is the cup used by the Queen mother when she popped into Mrs Atkinson's for tea yesterday. There is still the faintest trace of lipstick on the cup. 'I haven't washed it,' Mrs Atkinson told me. 'And I don't think I ever shall.' DAILY MIRROR

☐ As for the phrase 'Jewish bourgeois nationalist' this is a political characterization of the term Zionist and has no anti-semitic connotation whatever. DAILY WORKER

The mettle of the people

☐ Now that the war is over it is time our youth was thinking of something better than swing music and jazz bands for enjoyment. I suggest Band of Hope meetings and lantern lectures in wintertime and trips to old ruined castles and abbeys in summer. *A letter in the* NORTHERN ECHO

☐ When a Manchester man, with a handcart laden with bananas, had to go to the police station for causing an obstruction, his queue followed. LANCASHIRE DAILY POST

☐ Admiral Sir Geoffrey Layton, Commander-in-Chief, Portsmouth, at Hove on Saturday opened the swimming pool at the £170,000 King Alfred Baths by pushing two Wrens into the water. THE TIMES

☐ An attack on the Government's bread rationing scheme is made in this month's Felbridge Parish Magazine by the Rev. W. H. Hewitt (Vicar).

He writes: 'Our ink flows to you from a heart full of black perturbation through a pen shaking with deep indignation, conveying its message to eyes filled with consternation, because we live by bread – and bread is now rationed.' CRAWLEY AND DISTRICT OBSERVER

☐ Quite a number of young officers who have been demobilized want to wear bowler hats to show that they were young officers. 'It may well be that the bowler hat is getting to the top of the tree,' said Mr R. Weatherall, a master of Eton College. EVENING STANDARD

☐ On her 107th birthday, in August, she attributed her great age to a lifetime of hard work and the fact that she never had a boy friend. STAR

□ An Upwell (Norfolk) grocer unable to sell a new line of sweetened drinks, put them under the counter and recommended them to each customer individually. He sold out in a few hours. EVENING NEWS

□ Just before the war she became 'morally rearmed' by joining the Oxford Group and was photographed in a pink negligée with Dr Buchman. *From a report on Mae West*, NEWS CHRONICLE

□ The West Surrey Committee record the instance of a man who wished to take divorce proceedings, but later withdrew the application 'in case his wife got to hear about it'. *Annual Report, 1947, of the Law Society*

□ Engagement: George Harold Stiles Rome, only son of Mr S. G. Rome and Mrs Rome, Whatton Lodge, Gullane, East Lothian, and Marjorie Susan Mary Maclachlan of Machlachlan, eldest daughter of the late Maclachlan of Maclachlan and of Mrs Maclachlan of Maclachlan, Castle Lachlan, Strathlachlan, Argyll. WEEKLY SCOTSMAN

□ I have just come across a brilliant idea which I feel it my duty to pass on to all fathers immediately. It is nothing less than the perfect toy to keep children quiet! You put the child (age about three) in the bath and pour in a pound of sprats. *Letter in the* DAILY EXPRESS

□ Material misfortune seemed to dog him. He was half killed in an accident to the ambulance he served: his house was destroyed in the blitz and all his unsold pictures with it: he was employed by the BBC. *Introduction to Catalogue of Paintings at the Lefevre Gallery*

□ A marriage at Merthyr. Stipendiary magistrate to a woman who sought a maintenance order:

Do you love your husband?

No. I married him out of spite. I have been let down twice. I determined the next man who asked me had had it. DAILY GRAPHIC

□ 'He is in a very depressed state. He is contemplating marriage,' said the Deputy Chief Constable of a prisoner at Rochdale today. MANCHESTER EVENING NEWS

□ Judge Wethered granted a decree at Bristol Divorce Court to a man who, he said, found another man in his wife's bed partly clothed, eating a hot lunch. BRISTOL EVENING WORLD

□ The Great Wall of China, built between B.C. 228–210, is the oldest wall extant. In its own class, a Bronco toilet roll is also longest lasting because it contains approximately 700 sheets ... hundreds more than average. *Advertisement in* THE TIMES

□ Fined £2 at East Norton, Leicestershire, yesterday for exceeding the speed limit ... Mr — said he was so disgusted at receiving the summons that he had sacked five men and rejected a £3,000 export order. NEWS OF THE WORLD

□ Four 2-cwt. turtles, which will make soup for the Lord Mayor's banquet on 11 November, were each given six oysters and a bottle of champagne (Cordon Rouge, 1927) when they reached London by plane from Trinidad last night. 'The champagne warms the turtles and cheers them,' said Mr John Lusty, of the firm which will make the soup. DAILY EXPRESS

☐ Kipper sur Toast *From Lyons Corner House Menu*

☐ Vice-Admiral Sir John Edgell was speaking last night at the annual dinner of the Croydon branch of the Royal Naval Old Comrades' Association when he turned over his notes and stopped. Then he said, 'I'm afraid I shall have to end my speech here. By mistake I have brought the shopping-list my wife gave me this morning.' SUNDAY PICTORIAL

☐ English girls standing still in the nude will try to reproduce the atmosphere of the French show.

'But if they move a single inch,' Mr J. S. H. Partridge, chairman of the Entertainments Committee of the justices, warned yesterday, 'they may face the risk of prosecution by the police.' DAILY MAIL

☐ London Transport staff at Acton to-day found footprints on the freshly painted ceiling of an Underground carriage. They were investigating if a man could have walked upside down on the ceiling while strap-hanging. STAR

☐ When I pointed out the folly of a male shop assistant who was coughing and sneezing near an exposed keg of butter without using a handkerchief, the young lady serving me replied innocently: 'Oh, it isn't butter, it's margarine.' *Letter in the* SUNDAY DISPATCH

☐ A lead from the Corporation, a few pounds spent on gondolas, tables outside the waterside pubs, plenty of coloured lights, and Wigan, like Venice, could be taking in dollars from tourists. DAILY MIRROR

☐ To help people cope with modern civilization, the manufacture of aspirins on a large scale was demonstrated by Boots (Chemists). MANSFIELD REPORTER

☐ Solve Your Problem Ltd (Agency) urgently require office accommodation for own use; moderate rent. *Advertisement in* THE TIMES

☐ Ilkley is having one of the most successful Bank Holidays for years. Crowds have left a trail of litter on the riverside and moors. BRADFORD TELEGRAPH

☐ War in Korea and the rearmament programme have already affected timber prices and this will mean that Ice Lollie Sticks and Ice Cream Spoons will cost more. CONFECTIONERY JOURNAL

☐ Dr R. Leslie Ridge, chairman, told Middlesex executive committee of the Health Service, yesterday, that a set of false teeth was found stuck in a meringue behind a tree at Buckingham Palace after a garden party. DAILY EXPRESS

☐ Hotel-keepers and seaside caterers are watching the move made by Mr George Brenner, chairman of the Grand Pier Co., Weston-Super-Mare, who is investigating the possibility of legal action to restrain the BBC from broadcasting 'discouraging' weather forecasts. EVENING STANDARD

☐ An Alsatian dog bit a Communist candidate in a local election and licked the face of the policeman who came to investigate, Otley magistrates were told yesterday. NEWS CHRONICLE

□ A Nigerian told Islington Rent Tribunal that to secure a lease on premises in Holloway Road he had paid the owner about £250 in coconuts and cash. He added that he had given about £80 in cash and 3,200 coconuts. EVENING NEWS

□ Mr C. Adams, chairman of Walberswick, Suffolk, parish council, called a tittertorter a butterwats when he was a boy. 'I suppose most people call it a see-saw now,' he told the council yesterday. DAILY MAIL

□ From the funeral director's point of view, undertaking is a service industry: the raw material is supplied by the customer, processed according to the customer's order, and returned to the customer in finished form. CAMBRIDGE JOURNAL

□ The most cheerful reports, indeed, come from Wales, where the problem is not so much the amount of drinking that goes on in licensed houses but the amount of singing. In Caërnarvonshire, says the police report to the licensing justices, this singing has now reached 'serious proportions'. MANCHESTER GUARDIAN

□ 'Since the war the flea position has been getting steadily worse. I blame the vacuum cleaners and "new-fangled" disinfectants.' DAILY TELEGRAPH

□ An extra pair of trousers is to be issued to Tottenham's town hall keeper 'to uphold the dignity of the borough'. DAILY EXPRESS

□ Remove the bedclothes gently. Take a piece of damp soap and dab on to the flea. This prevents it escaping. THE 'OLIO' COOKERY BOOK

□ Could not cups of strong tea be called the English *vin du pays*? SUNDAY TIMES

□ The most serious of these offences are punishable by death, and some of them carry heavier penalties when committed on active service. AIRMAN'S GUIDE

□ Councillor Courts said he only hoped it was a Rembrandt and then they could sell it and help pay for the public conveniences so badly needed. TAMWORTH HERALD

□ How to make a cup of tea after an atom bomb attack, is one of the Civil Defence lessons being given to South-East London housewives. STAR

□ The Evening of Clairvoyance on Tuesday, 4 December at 7 p.m. has been cancelled owing to unforeseen circumstances. *Notice in the* EAST KENT TIMES

□ The R.H.S. memorandum makes the further very sensible suggestion that the term 'bastard trenching' should now be dropped, as the more pleasing term 'double digging' means exactly the same thing. AMATEUR GARDENING

□ 'There seems to be no code of conduct among young burglars,' says Lord Keyes, who will be 33 in March. 'In the old days there were gentlemen burglars. The police tell me that some of these older men are seriously disturbed at the way these younger men go on.' EVENING STANDARD

□ People who find it necessary to vomit whilst in a railway carriage should discreetly use their hats; this would come naturally to anyone properly brought up. *Letter in the* PICTURE POST

□ While I pondered in a restaurant over my choice of soup the waitress said that the brown soup (6d.) kidney (6d.) and the oxtail (9d.) were all from the same pot. The difference in name and price, she said, was 'to add a little variety to the menu'. *Letter in the* SUNDAY EXPRESS

□ Private McNally would have beaten 2nd Lieut. Hoppe for the Army cruiser-weight championship had he not so obviously suffered from an understandable psychological reluctance to hit an officer. *Letter in the* SUNDAY GRAPHIC

□ Every time I see an early tulip, upright as a soldier of the Queen, I lift my chin and straighten my shoulders. *Letter in the* EVENING NEWS

□ The names of comics which glorify vice, brutality, sadism and sex are to be circulated to Scout leaders. BALHAM AND TOOTING NEWS AND MERCURY

□ So determined was I that my two young sons should grow up, their mouths unsullied by swear words, that I consulted a psychologist. He said that if I swore freely in front of them, swearing would cease to have any novelty for them and they would not be interested. He was right. My boys do not swear, but I am inextricably in the grip of the swearing habit. *Letter in* REYNOLDS' NEWS

□ Gents Braces 4/11, Mens Braces 2/11 *Sign in a Nottingham store*

□ Civic luncheons of stew and steamed jam pudding cooked in an old dustbin, will be served at a Civil Defence emergency feeding exhibition at Hatley Heath, West Bromwich. SUNDAY DISPATCH

□ Asked in Leigh today if he could pay a 20s fine and two guineas costs for maliciously wounding his wife with a poker, a man replied: 'You will have to ask the missus. I have no money.' MANCHESTER EVENING NEWS

□ If we are ever to have peace we must think of the people in Communist countries as human beings. And we do not do that. ... I remember a friend showing me a snapshot of a little Russian boy picking his nose. Somehow, it was a revelation to me. *Letter in the* LISTENER

□ The Unit was born after films of drill on a six-inch gun had shown that No. 6 'stood stiffly to attention at the back of the gun, doing absolutely nothing'. No reason could be found for this until a sergeant-major of the Boer War recalled that No. 6 had been the man who used to hold the horses. MANCHESTER GUARDIAN

□ Mutual trust seems to grow more naturally between people who have attended the same school, fagged for and flogged one another. NEWS CHRONICLE

Women again

□ Do not forget the little woollen panties, which can be as light as a feather, as pretty as silk, but as warm as toast, and far more conducive to a wild rose flush than silk scanties which encourage a mauvish tint instead. *Article in the* NEWS CHRONICLE

□ And if you feel exotic and extravagant you *could* have some tiny jewelled nose clips. WOMAN AND BEAUTY

□ The modeller calls this 'The H-bomb Style', explaining that the 'H' is for peroxide of hydrogen, used for the colouring. The hair is dressed to rise in waves, as from a bomb-burst, at the nape of the neck. DAILY TELEGRAPH

□ Check up in advance that you have all the things you need for a quick transformation either in your handbag or your desk drawer. You'll want: cleansing lotion, cotton wool, tissues, toothbrush, toothpaste, nail brush, soap, deodorizing tablets, eye lotion, eye bath, foundation, matching powder, make-up brush, eye shadow, mascara with two brushes, lipstick, lipbrush, cologne perfume, clothes brush. WOMANS OWN

The administration in action

□ Railways this year will be able to carry double the number of pigeons they did in 1954. *Report in the* DAILY DESPATCH

□ A West Suffolk farmer, who has applied to the Air Ministry for the derequisitioning of 250 acres of land for the spring sowing of wheat, has received notice of the release of a square foot of soil. *Report in the* DAILY TELEGRAPH

□ THE FREEDOM OF BURY
Bury General Purposes Committee have set up a special sub-committee to make arrangements for granting the freedom of the borough to the Lancashire Fusiliers on 3 August. Other corporation committees will 'entertain' the soldiers by offering for three days free plunge and slipper baths, free travel on the buses and trams, an art gallery lecture on the town's history, and a visit to the town's sewage works. MANCHESTER EVENING NEWS

□ An official of the Ministry of Food stated in London last night: 'On the first application it was stated that Taylor was suffering from malnutrition. We were advised that a person suffering from this complaint did not require extra rations, so the application was refused.' DAILY MAIL

□ In pursuance of the Sunday ban on darts in public houses, Sheffield police yesterday paid surprise visits to houses, and in one case a game of darts in progress was immediately stopped. SHEFFIELD STAR

□ Councillor Jacques's plea for the gates of Barwell Recreation Ground to be left open on Sunday received Council approval, but it was decided to chain up the swing lest children be

tempted to use them on the Sabbath.
HINCKLEY TIMES AND GUARDIAN

☐ The Chairman, Mr A. Woodley, referring to Great Missenden, said: 'In May, 1944, the Ministry refused an application to build cottages because it was said the washing might be seen by the Prime Minister on his way to Chequers.' EVENING STANDARD

☐ Newquay (Cornwall) Council, wishing to repair some of the boats on their children's boating lake, applied to the Board of Trade for a licence to use 16 cubic feet of timber for the purpose. The Board of Trade has returned their application and told them it should have been sent to the Admiralty. DAILY TELEGRAPH

☐ Temporary Lieutenant John Thomas Wardle, of H.M.S. *Lochinvar*, was ordered by a naval court-martial at Rosyth today to forfeit three months seniority, to be dismissed from H.M.S. *Lochinvar* and severely reprimanded.

He pleaded guilty to taking his lunch and drinking with five ratings on Christmas day aboard the minesweeper he commanded. EVENING STANDARD

☐ Owing to the fuel crisis officials are advised to take advantage of their typists between the hours of 12 and 2. *Notice posted inside the Town Hall of a London borough*

☐ Supervising the work were Catchment Board officials and Army officers. 'We feel that we are fighting a winning battle,' one official told me. 'We shall go on feeling that we are winning until we have lost.' NEWS CHRONICLE

☐ From today the price of rice and rice products will be increased slightly. But there will still be none in the shops, say the Ministry of Food. DAILY MAIL

☐ A Glasgow clothing firm has reduced its consumption of gas to such an extent that yesterday a man who called from the municipal gas department said the meter would have to be taken away. Surprised at the low reading of the meter, he was told the firm had been economizing in response to the Ministry of Fuel appeal. 'That is overdoing it,' he remarked. DAILY TELEGRAPH

☐ Following a complaint by Chesham Council, Buckinghamshire County Council have made a bye-law prohibiting the barking of dogs at night. NEWS CHRONICLE

☐ No one has applied for the £1,000-a-year job as psychiatrist to Stoke-on-Trent Education Committee. Mr H. Barks said at yesterday's meeting that the job should be filled quickly before psychiatry went out of fashion. DAILY EXPRESS

☐ Lavatories, he said, would produce revenue. Cemeteries used to produce revenue but did not seem to produce so much. He thought that priority could be given to lavatories. *Report of a Town Council meeting in the* WORTHING HERALD

☐ The Minister of Defence says that efforts are being made to prevent such things as a three-ton lorry being used to convey a latch-key. BATH AND WILTS CHRONICLE AND HERALD

☐ Two men arrested for trying to buy gold from a supposed black-marketeer who turned out to be a police inspector, have been released after proving that they too were police inspectors masquerading as black-market operators. EDINBURGH EVENING DISPATCH

☐ After inquiries the police searched both hearse and coffin before allowing the vehicle to proceed. The reason they gave was that previously they had seen another hearse, complete with flowers, pass through a village several times. Eventually they noted that the flowers were withering. They had stopped the hearse and ordered the coffin to be opened, and in it found four sides of bacon destined for the London black market. THE TIMES

☐ The Home Secretary has abolished the regulations, hitherto prevalent in certain Provincial Police Forces, prohibiting officers, except with prior consent of the Chief Constable, from marrying, playing cards, unbuttoning their tunics in canteens or consulting a solicitor. *Law Society's* GAZETTE

☐ For the purpose of this part of this schedule a person over pensionable age, not being an insured person, shall be treated as an employed person if he would be an insured person were he under pensionable age and would be an employed person were he an insured person. *National Insurance Bill, 1st Schedule*

☐ Nothing proves the desire of the Festival Club to be helpful more than the bilingual notice which hangs on the telephone kiosk in the vestibule. Above is the word 'Telephone'; underneath is the word 'Téléphone'. SCOTSMAN

☐ Letter from a furniture manufacturer to a customer:
'Further to your esteemed order for 20 medium oak chairs, the Board of Trade halved the order and only sanctioned ten. Will you, therefore, please submit a further order for 20 chairs, so that the Board of Trade can halve same and so give us the requisite number of chairs?' EVENING NEWS

☐ A man walked into a public assistance office, picked up a chair and smashed eight windows while three Civil Servants just stood by and watched, a court was told yesterday. The officials explained that they were not allowed to lay hands on anyone seeking assistance. DAILY MIRROR

☐ Counsel appearing for the War Office at an inquest this week said he had been instructed: 'The Secretary for War wishes to express his deep regret at this tragedy [an Army motor-cyclist knocked down and killed a Bermondsey man]. The Secretary is deeply disturbed that his department should be concerned in any way with the shortening of human life.' SOUTH LONDON PRESS

☐ Corned beef was sent to a Bridgend school canteen. Teachers sniffed it and did not like it. A canteen manageress sniffed it but pronounced it good; the town sanitary inspector sniffed it and passed it as good; the town medical officer sniffed it and declared it good – then ordered it to be destroyed because too many people had sniffed it. DAILY EXPRESS

☐ Hastings and St Leonards Rowing Club, after being granted a road transport permit for the conveyance of a racing boat from Hastings to Hammersmith for slight modifications, have been refused a road transport permit to bring it back again. SUNDAY GRAPHIC

☐ Macclesfield Education Finance Sub-committee allowed pay to a male teacher for one day's absence to attend the funeral of his mother-in-law. They refused it to a woman teacher who attended the funeral of her father-in-law. DAILY TELEGRAPH

Religious guidance

☐ Clothing worn by the rural dean of Bletchley, the Rev. C. A. Wheeler, caught fire during a clergymen's service in Leighton Buzzard parish church yesterday. The back of the surplice was set alight by a candle while a hymn which referred to 'the consuming flames of sin' was being sung. The flames enveloped the back of the surplice without the rural dean noticing it. THE TIMES

☐ On the north wall there is a large painting of the Trinity in which the figure of the Almighty is about life-size . . . *Letter to* THE TIMES

☐ At both Services in the morning it is intended to preach a series of sermons on the 'Deadly Sins' omitting lust. OUR CHURCH REVIEW

☐ Sherry, pet cat of the Bishop of Colchester, has been renamed Shandy. 'One of my clergy suggested Sherry was a little too strong,' the Bishop explained. PEOPLE

☐ The bishops stand outside party politics. Most bishops could be described as Liberal Conservatives, with strong Socialist leanings. BIRMINGHAM MAIL

☐ The Vicar of Bracknell (Berks), the Rev. J. E. J. Esher, suggests the birch and the 'cat' as preliminaries to divorce proceedings. In that way, he tells his parishioners, we should go far to stay the rot. NEWS CHRONICLE

☐ 'We derive our inspiration from God, but we are grateful to *The Times* for the strengthening of our convictions.' *Bishop of Carlisle's address to a Diocesan Conference*

□ Any of these office holders, if alert, may ask his Bishop to make him Dean Emeritus, Archdeacon Emeritus, or Canon Emeritus, upon his retirement. This enables ex-Deans and ex-Archdeacons to retain their gaiters and other accoutrements that stamp them as men of rank in the hierarchy. It is a heavy fall, with great loss of face, to go about in plain trousers (even if worn with bicycle clips) after having worn gaiters and shown a fine calf for many years. PARSON & PARISH

□ Dr Morris, addressing his annual diocesan conference at Monmouth, said it was wrong to think that Henry VIII set a royal example for divorce. He was never divorced; in the two cases where his wife was not killed the marriages were annulled. NEWS CHRONICLE

□ The account of religious terms towards the end of the book has been rearranged so that dissenters and nonconformists are no longer grouped with idolators, fire worshippers and other heathens. *From the Introduction to the new 'Everyman' edition of Roget's* THESAURUS

The Law's helping hand

□ Capt. E. C. Pinckney, Chairman of the Bradford-on-Avon magistrates, yesterday told a man who three times protested that he knew he would never get justice in the court and wanted to be tried by a jury: 'There is such a thing as contempt of Court. So if you do not want to go to gaol straight away keep your head shut. I have never heard such blasted rubbish in all my life.' NEWS CHRONICLE

□ Asked why he signed a confession of the offences at the Police Station, Clark replied, 'I thought you always had to sign if a police officer told you to.' ESSEX COUNTY STANDARD

□ Leslie Gordon Waterman, aged 32, a golf caddie, of Hampreston, Dorset, was sentenced to nine months' imprisonment for stealing 126 golf balls and committing bigamy with Irene Harrop. NEWS OF THE WORLD

□ It is the very merit of the death penalty that its bark is worse than its bite. *Letter from Lord Quickswood in the* DAILY TELEGRAPH

□ In ninety-nine cases out of a hundred, said the judge, a man who runs away is guilty, but X was the innocent one per cent. ... Mrs Y had no right to shout, 'Stop that man' when he bolted. ... She could have called out, 'Will you please stop that gentleman, and kindly ask him to give me his name and address as he has just assaulted me.' DAILY MIRROR

□ 'This form was drawn up in 1936, and it does not clearly state what is meant. It is just a legal document.' DAILY MAIL

□ Judge — said the conduct of the defendant was disgusting. 'That any man could hit a girl who wears glasses is beyond my comprehension.' EVENING NEWS

□ The magistrate, Mr Harley, said he thought it proper that at times a man should beat his wife, and the Bible supported that statement; but beating must be done as a service of love, not in temper. Accused should have used a reasonably sized stick. It was a pity he lost his temper and used an iron bar. DAILY TELEGRAPH

□ Fining them the maximum of £10 each, Mrs M. A. Cumelia, presiding magistrate, said: 'I think you might have been reading a certain Sunday newspaper and got into your head ideas that you could both wisely lose. If you had not come from good homes we would have authorized the Press to publish your names.' NEWS CHRONICLE

□ At King's Lynn, Norfolk, yesterday, a man was granted legal aid when he chose to go for trial on a charge of making a false statement for the purpose of obtaining free legal aid. DAILY HERALD

Man's best friends

☐ If foxes could hear all sides in the debate on hunting, I think they would vote solidly for its continuance. THE FIELD

☐ The snail watchers are interested in snails from all angles. They search literature and art for reference. At the moment they are investigating the snail's reaction to music. 'We have played to them on the harp in the garden and in the country on the pipe,' said Mr Heaton, 'and we have taken them into the house and played to them on the piano.' STAR

☐ We find that our cows give their highest milk yields to the strains of eighteenth-century chamber music, such as Haydn quartets. Music in the modern idiom often calms them into lying down at the wrong time; 'swing' definitely creates a 'kicking the bucket' tendency. *Letter in the* RADIO TIMES

☐ Asked at Bedlington (Northumberland) juvenile court today to value his bantam hen stolen by boys, a 60-year-old witness replied: 'As a bird I value it at 5s., but as a friend I value it as 7s. 6d.' MANCHESTER EVENING CHRONICLE

☐ I am convinced that if a fox could vote, he would vote Tory. *Letter in the* SUSSEX EXPRESS AND COUNTY HERALD

☐ A South Devon hotel brochure announces: 'Guests' dogs are charged 1s. or 1s. 6d. per day according to size and social standing.' DAILY EXPRESS

☐ Performing mice are to demonstrate the correct use of zebra crossings at Tredegar, Monmouthshire, during National Road Safety Week. DAILY DISPATCH

□ Protesting against unrestricted shooting of seabirds off the French Coast which is being advertised by the French Railways, Miss Nash Thomas said, at Ickenham Natural History Society A.G.M. on Friday, that these would, in fact, be British birds feeding on foreign soil. UXBRIDGE WEEKLY POST

□ An entirely new development is the taking over the care of their own infants by young mothers of the aristocratic and cultivated sorts who have never before in history actually nursed their babies, though they have been expert and successful in the raising and training of animals. LADY

□ Canine chastity belts are on sale at a well-known London store. Part plastic shield, part leather harness, the contrivance is made in six sizes and costs 24s. 11d. The makers claim 'maximum protection with minimum anxiety'. SUNDAY DISPATCH

4

The New Elizabethan Age. Queen Elizabeth ascends the throne in 1952, and Britain searches for a new role as a second-class nation, while the Big Powers explode their H-bombs and race for the moon. Roger Bannister runs the first mile in under four minutes, Jim Laker takes 19 wickets in a Test Match, and Alf Ramsey pulls in the World Cup for England's footballers. Sir Harold Macmillan tells his people they have never had it so good, and then Harold Wilson launches a technocratic society. Britain acclaimed as inventor of mini-cars and mini-skirts.

☐ The many forces that have suffered defeat at the hands of the British soldier with all his crudities appear to prefer to be defeated by him rather than by any army in the world. *Letter in* THE TIMES

☐ All through this it was possible to notice the difference in character between Lenin and Stalin. Lenin was in many respects more British. MANCHESTER GUARDIAN

☐ All U.N.O. can do is to pass resolutions. When these are directed at Britain they have no moral force and should be treated with contempt. *Editorial in the* DAILY EXPRESS

☐ I think at the present time when our nation finds it is in difficulties it has always been our habit and reputation not to argue about the thing but to put our heads down and shout, and I think this is the thing we ought to do today. *Letter in the* BUCKS EXAMINER

☐ Lord Hailsham said that earth satellites in the wrong hands could cause disaster instead of being a great boon.
The satellite was largely the product of Russian scientist Peter Kapitza, who was educated at Cambridge. So it was largely a triumph of British education. EVENING STANDARD

☐ After a young Italian had walked up to one of his customers, pulled him to the ground and kicked his head, an Angmering petrol pump attendant took him aside and told him, 'We don't do these things in England.' LITTLEHAMPTON GAZETTE

☐ The Government wants to change our money system. But half the world's trade is done in pounds, shillings and pence. Instead of Britain switching to decimal coinage, why don't the foreigners change to sterling? DAILY EXPRESS

☐ In reply to Olga Franklin on square meals, the reason why the French mess everything about in casseroles and suchlike dishes is they cannot procure the quality of meat obtainable in Britain; and they wouldn't know how to cook it anyway. *Letter in the* DAILY MAIL

☐ A woman when asked her religion at Tower Bridge Court today before taking the oath replied, 'British'. EVENING NEWS

☐ Into this eager void came – the world's principal human being. Her Majesty the Queen. NEWS CHRONICLE

The ruling class

□ It is explained that, for convenience and brevity, the term Communist is used to cover Communist and Fascist alike. *Reply by Mr Enoch Powell, Financial Secretary to the Treasury, reported in* THE TIMES

□ Flashing her hazel eyes Lady Harding said: 'It really is a pity you know, this trouble. Cyprus is a tourists' paradise. And the people are so healthy.' DAILY EXPRESS

□ Later a woman called from the bank. 'Thank you for the fly,' she said. 'It improved sport a lot.'

The woman was Queen Elizabeth, the Queen Mother. My friend was startled, but even so, standing in the river, she curtsied. SUNDAY PICTORIAL

□ Princess Anne is reported to be alarmingly unafraid of horses. She has been seen to wander up nervelessly to very large horses who are not aware of her royal status. DAILY EXPRESS

□ Councillor F. W. Nash, of Castle Rising, Norfolk, has been returned unopposed to the seat on Freedridge Lynn council which had been declared vacant on the grounds that he had not attended meetings regularly. DAILY HERALD

□ Mr Tom Williamson, the general secretary of the National Union of General and Municipal Workers ... denied the charge that trade union leaders were out of touch with the rank and file, and said it was the rank and file which was out of touch with the leadership. MANCHESTER GUARDIAN

□ 'I think that at the present time, more than any other, it is more important that ex-Servicemen should get together over the Middle East and Far East

than all the politicians, who know nothing about the Middle East, the Far East, nor any other East, for politicians don't know Orientals like we do – they don't know that the only way to deal with them is to kick their backsides,' said Brigadier M. F. Farquharson-Roberts. DERBY EVENING TELEGRAPH

□ If Princess Margaret is lightly to be allowed to marry the man she loves a grave blow will have been struck at the sanctity of marriage, already hard-pressed by decaying moral standards. PEOPLE

□ Nowadays, if you are worried about seating arrangements for your guests,

you can write to the Heralds of the College of Arms and hope for a reply as superb as the one received by the anxious hostess of the Aga Khan. 'The Aga Khan,' it ran, 'is held by his followers to be the direct descendant of God. An English Duke takes precedence.' HOUSEWIFE

□ If hydrogen bombs were exploded over this country, he added, we should all be involved in a complete transformation of our way of life. *Sir Hugh Lucas-Tooth opening a C.D. headquarters, reported in the* SUNDAY DISPATCH

□ What I have said has demonstrated that it is very difficult to find an answer to that question, but if I were pressed for an answer I would say that, so far as we can see, taking it rather by and large, taking one thing with another, and taking the average of Departments, it is probable that there would not be found to be very much in it either way. *Sir Thomas Padmore, reported in Minutes of Evidence to the Royal Commission on the Civil Service*

□ Lord Saye and Sele, in a maiden speech, said the hereditary system was the only method of selecting a body of people which was completely unbiased. Every other method, except perhaps lottery, must depend on somebody's opinion. THE TIMES

□ Mr Clement Davies was also in first-class form. His forthright declaration that 'you are either a Liberal or you are not a Liberal' brought down the house. Everybody knew what he meant! *A. J. Cummings in the* NEWS CHRONICLE

□ Socialist government consists in the application of Socialist principles, while Conservative government subsists, or ought to, in the application of divine law. *Letter in the* PEEBLESSHIRE NEWS

□ The first Californian prunes, part of £2,000,000 worth of fruit to be exchanged for US rocket bases in Britain, have just arrived in this country. DAILY EXPRESS

□ The Queen was escorted up a gentle, red-carpeted ramp which, like all the passages and stairwells she used, had been sprayed with scent.

'We did not spray the stables,' said a Jockey Club member, 'since we were informed that the Queen liked the smell of horses.' DAILY EXPRESS

□ 'For the past ten years I have been driving in Birmingham and have always found the city's police absolutely wonderful.

'But this young constable seemed all out to be unpleasant. He didn't realize I was a titled person driving my wife, the Marchioness, to address a meeting of 1,000 members of the Salvation Army.

'I suppose it was because we were using the smallest of our fleet of cars.' DAILY MIRROR

□ Miss Lennox-Boyd, sister of the man with Cyprus on his shoulders, is equally single-minded.

'I'm sick of hearing about consciences,' she said fiercely. 'What we want is a real Conservative who doesn't keep seeing good in the other side.' SUNDAY DISPATCH

□ Major S. G. Grant, the association's chairman, states firmly that they will not demand from their new candidate, whoever he may be, any categorical assurance of complete subservience to the association's views. 'Every M.P. like any other Englishman, has the right to his own opinions,' he remarks. Their objection is not to Mr Nicolson using his own judgement. They dislike the judgement he used. THE TIMES

□ The Earl of Home, Secretary of State for Commonwealth Relations, introducing the Pakistan Prime Minister, said: 'He coxed his college boat at Oxford – and I'm told he sings Gilbert and Sullivan in his bath, which immediately makes us take him to our hearts.' EVENING STANDARD

□ I have heard it said of the 'backwoods' peer that he had three qualities. He knew how to kill a fox, he knew how to get rid of a bad tenant, and he knew how to discard an unwanted mistress. A man who possesses these three qualities would certainly have something to contribute to the work of the House. *Lord Winster reported in the* MANCHESTER GUARDIAN

□ Blenheim is a famous showplace, but the Duke can often relax enough to throw raspberries to the ceiling in the fabulous dining hall and catch them in his mouth. 'I know by the applause when he's at it', says the Duchess. SHE

□ Lady Huggins, vice-chairman of the Conservative Commonwealth Council, declared at Nottingham University last night that too much fuss was being made of the deaths of Mau Mau detainees at Hola Camp, Kenya. 'These men were undoubtedly beaten to death but they were in fact the worst type of criminals themselves and they would not have been accepted back in their home districts.' NOTTINGHAM GUARDIAN JOURNAL

□ One person who watched the result of the Kinross by-election today with pride as well as interest is Mrs Florence Hill, who was Sir Alec Douglas-Home's under-nurse when he was one year old. ... 'I had to see that Master Alec didn't talk to the servants,' she recalls, 'and that he didn't leave our part of the house.' EVENING STANDARD

□ Lady Delacombe, tall, handsome and forthright, has been First British Lady of the West's shopfront city for the past two and a half years.

'I love it in Berlin,' she said. 'We are all better housed here than we were in the Zone – and we were well enough housed there. Gin is only 8s. 6d. a bottle – or something like that. And even other ranks' wives are permitted a maid.' GUARDIAN

□ The perils of travelling without a valet are illustrated by an experience which recently befell the Duke of Marlborough as a guest of one of his daughters. She was surprised to hear him complain that his toothbrush 'did not foam properly' so would she buy him a new one. He had to be reminded gently that without the aid of tooth-powder, usually applied for him each morning by his valet, no toothbrush foamed automatically. SUNDAY TELEGRAPH

□ We turned to the Life Peers. Mr Townsend said: 'Some of them seem to think that because they are life peers their lineage doesn't matter. Florence Horsburgh's like that. But Lord Peddie, the Co-op chief, gave us a delightful surprise. His family goes back to 1800. An excellent show for a Co-op man.' *Editor of* BURKE'S PEERAGE, *reported in the* SUNDAY EXPRESS

□ Duncan Sandys was born to command. He was educated at Eton and Oxford where he studied some, worked his golf handicap down to seven, and was given an Indian servant by his father for his 21st birthday. NEWSWEEK

□ Said Mr Profumo: 'I do not think anything will give the Russians a better idea of our democratic way of life than having a look at the Queen on her birthday, surrounded by some of the most valiant troops in the world.' DAILY MAIL

□ From his home in Broadway, Worcs., yesterday, Sir Gerald said to me: 'I certainly did not intend to be offensive in any way about coloured people. I regard 'big buck nigger' as a complimentary expression, not derogatory. Nigger means Negro; buck means large, masculine, manly.' SUNDAY TELEGRAPH

☐ Where Mr Macmillan always stalked any solution, pondering problems from every viewpoint often for hours on end, Sir Alec tends to make his mind up more quickly, an ability less the result of any great natural skill, but from amazing economy of thought. EAST ANGLIAN DAILY TIMES

☐ No, the Labour Party's moral attitude simply does not stand up, because this country, as a trading nation, cannot afford to take a moral line. *Lord Lambton in the* EVENING STANDARD

☐ It is about time a nicer word than 'Commoner' was found for those who are not of noble blood. It is particularly unpleasant to see this word continually used to describe Mr Antony Armstrong-Jones. *Letter in the* DAILY MIRROR

☐ 'My favourite programme,' said the Queen Mother, on a later occasion, when the conversation turned to radio, 'is "Mrs Dale's Diary". I try never to miss it because it is the only way of knowing what goes on in a middle-class family.' EVENING NEWS

☐ The Queen's detective, Superintendent Albert Edward Perkins, was not so fortunate. He managed to get his rolled umbrella securely caught in the harness of his elephant as he climbed up the ladder, and to the amusement of the Queen had great difficulty in getting himself, briefcase, grey Homburg hat and the umbrella into position.

☐ Over the past few weeks all English people have been thinking of how best we can remember Sir Winston Churchill. May I suggest a way? I think Prince Charles should eventually marry one of Sir Winston's female granddaughters, and so the Churchill family can be loved along with our royal family. *Letter in the* BOLTON EVENING NEWS

☐ At a two-roomed cottage near Glamis Castle, a white-haired mother spoke proudly yesterday of a little service she had been able to give the Royal Family. She revealed that 34 years ago she agreed to her baby son taking the birth registration number of 13 so that it should not go to Princess Margaret. SUNDAY EXPRESS

☐ Lew Grade, managing director of Associated Tele-Vision, the London weekend company, said today: 'We are not going to ask the researchers to tell us what programme to do, but once we have made up our minds about a programme we want to know if we are putting on stuff that is inane or nonsense.' EVENING STANDARD

☐ Lord Mansfield, Lord Lieutenant of Perthshire, said in Perth today that he would like to see offenders finding things a lot less comfortable. 'I would like to see things like the treadmill introduced once again,' he said. THE TIMES

☐ Other gifts were more utilitarian. The American Government sent 25 ambulances, Nigeria £10,000 for national development. We gave a silver and gilt inkstand inscribed 'From Britain to Zambia, 1964'. DAILY TELEGRAPH

☐ The Burmese Army and the RAF searched for three days. No trace was found of it ... Princess Alexandra's teddy bear. Apparently she told her host in Mandalay she remembered taking teddy to bed. And now – Gone. Princess Alexandra is 25 this month. REYNOLDS NEWS

103

□ I remember the morning when he was taken exceedingly ill. Instead of the usual nod of the head to me on my arrival he spoke. 'Cronin,' he said, 'I think I'm dying.'

The habit of years could not be broken in me and I knew that Lord Tredegar in his more collected moments would not wish it to be. So correctly I replied, 'Very good, my lord' – and thereafter the normal silence between us was re-established to our mutual satisfaction. *Cronin's memoirs in the* PEOPLE

□ In order to improve on this performance in future overspill schemes, the Ministry of Housing, the Greater London Council and the Ministry of Labour were going through the machinery for decanting people with a fine toothcomb, Mr Mellish said. GUARDIAN

□ Mr Lionel Cox, Secretary of the Hull Fishing Vessel Owners' Association and the Hull Fishing Industry Association, who agreed to answer some of the men's complaints, said: 'People do get swept overboard, but they often get swept back again.' SUNDAY TIMES

□ One of Mrs Castle's sternest critics – 'a man from the motor trade' – unwittingly put his finger on the nub of the argument when he said: 'It's very difficult to discuss this with her rationally. You can produce a hundred and one good reasons against breathalysers. But when she started all this emotional talk about the number of lives it has saved you feel the ground being knocked away under your feet.' OBSERVER

□ The British representative at the Panmunjom commission, Brigadier Bancroft, remarked: 'The Koreans are fantastically anti-communist. They begin to learn their anti-communism in the school and then in the army. And by the time a chap has finished his national service he's a pretty anti-communist chap. They know they're allowed to think for themselves here and they know that in the North people are told what to think.' SUNDAY TIMES

□ A reader's assertion that Jesus and the Church have nothing in common is as ridiculous as saying that Harold Wilson and the Labour Party have nothing in common. *Letter in the* LEICESTER MERCURY

□ There is a nice old-fashioned answer to the old-fashioned game of rioting. It is to call out troops and a magistrate. Have him read the Riot Act, and if the mob does not disperse, shoot the ringleaders. *Letter in the* SUNDAY TELEGRAPH

□ Bro. Bill Carron will not be lost to the Labour Movement on his retirement. ... He will join the many other worthy workers who have entered the House of Lords with Life Peerages in an attempt to democratize the chamber of privilege. The good wishes of the General Secretary, Executive Council and members go with him in this new battle for the rights of the working class. AEU JOURNAL

□ It begins at about 7 a.m. We have breakfast together, and I talk while my husband reads the newspapers. *Mrs Wilson, quoted in the* DAILY EXPRESS

□ 'I'm glad to know there are rich people about. It affects me like looking at sunsets, and snow-capped mountains.' *Enoch Powell interviewed in the* DAILY MAIL

□ A spokesman at Buckingham Palace denied that the Prince would be beating the incomes freeze. 'It is not that sort of income,' he said. 'It simply means that he will get a larger share of the revenue from his estates than he did previously.' SUNDAY EXPRESS

□ Since the present government came in we have won the World Cup and Eurovision Song Contest. That should silence the knockers. *Letter in the* DAILY MIRROR

□ There was a hitch in the arrangements about the car in which the Queen and the Duke should drive. Corsican officials found a car they considered splendid enough for the occasion. Then they discovered that the car's owner had been divorced. It was thought that the Queen might be embarrassed over that. SUNDAY EXPRESS

The social pattern

□ A public house licencee told Bedford Bankruptcy Court yesterday that since he was made bankrupt the business had grown considerably because people came to see what a bankrupt looked like. DAILY EXPRESS

□ Seats in public lavatories in Bath are being stamped with a secret code letter to help police recognize any that are stolen. SUNDAY PICTORIAL

□ A man I know locks up his alarm clock in a tin medicine chest (for extra noise) every night before retiring.

To reach the key to open the chest to turn off the alarm he has to plunge his arm into a deep jug full of icy water where he dropped the key the night before. This is the only way he knows to be certain of waking up. SUNDAY GRAPHIC

□ I noticed that income tax demand notes are always addressed to me as 'Mr'.

When, however, it is a matter of surtax, I am addressed as 'Esq.' *Letter in the* DAILY TELEGRAPH

□ In Stafford Gaol Fuchs was put to work on kit-bags for the Army. Within a day he had discovered, by making a mathematical calculation, that the cloth could be cut a different way and the Government saved several thousand pounds a year. For this he was given a 2d.-a-week rise. EVENING NEWS

□ Your front page article about Africans being shot made me feel sick. Could not this kind of story be condensed and made more pleasant? *Letter in the* DAILY MIRROR

□ A spokesman of one advertising firm which has specialized in lingerie advertisements, told the *Daily Mirror* yesterday: 'What we want are girls who look like bishops' daughters and who can pose in revealing undies without losing a jot of respectability.' DAILY MIRROR

☐ Huddersfield Corporation is offering a reward of £20 for information leading to the arrest of the persons who took plants out of the flower beds in Greenhead Park on Friday night and scattered them on the paths. The bed which was most seriously damaged contained 33,350 plants arranged to depict a wastepaper basket and the words, 'Please use the litter baskets'. MANCHESTER GUARDIAN

☐ Sculptor Henry Moore has been asked not to leave any holes in which boys could trap their heads when he carves 'Family Group' for Harlow new town. NEWS CHRONICLE

☐ On the same bus as myself was a schoolboy, whose head had become stuck in a vase. His mother was rushing him off to hospital. Presumably to avoid attracting attention she had placed her son's school cap on top of the vase. *Letter in* JOHN BULL

☐ For months 80-year-old Bert Jackson has promised himself the first drink at a new club being built near his home at Edenthorpe, Doncaster. But a few weeks before the club was opened he died. ... Today his widow, Mrs Edith Jackson, will take a pint of beer in a lemonade bottle – the first drawn at the club – to the cemetery where her husband is buried. She plans to pour it over his grave – to fulfil Bert's promise. NEWS CHRONICLE

☐ Women in the Essex village of Ugley have changed the name of their organization from the Ugley Women's Institute to The Women's Institute (Ugley branch). NEWS CHRONICLE

☐ Air Ministry experts lead by 112 points to 111 in their August weather forecasting duel with Mr Harry Boon, of Cleethorpes, whose guide is the behaviour of gnats. NEWS CHRONICLE

☐ 'Capital punishment applied to the wrong type of child – the nervous, sensitive type – may do irreparable harm,' he said *Report of speech in the* NEWCASTLE JOURNAL

☐ I strongly object to being described as 'a woman'. When used by newspaper reporters, this term has a certain stigma attached to it. I am a young lady, well educated and refined, and a highbrow of the first order. *Letter in the* CATERHAM AND WARLINGHAM TIMES

☐ There is, I am sure, for most of us, a special pleasure in sinking your teeth into a peach produced on the estate of an earl who is related to the Royal Family. *Columnist in the* DAILY EXPRESS

☐ A school edition of *Hamlet*, in use in the Midlands of England, changes Shakespeare's 'Enter a bloody sergeant' to 'Enter a bleeding captain'. SCOTTISH COMMUNITY DRAMA ASSOCIATION BULLETIN

☐ Miss Vane submitted her poses to the Lord Chamberlain's Office for passing in the usual way. In one series she wore the peep-toe shoes and nothing else. The Lord Chamberlain ruled that the peep-toe shoes must be removed. SOUTH LONDON ADVERTISER

☐ I ventured in a big London restaurant the other day to compliment the waitress on the high standard they maintained. 'No,' she answered, 'you'll never find any cracked crockery used in here. Why, the moment a cup is cracked it is sent up at once to the staff canteen.' *Letter in the* MANCHESTER GUARDIAN

☐ The teenager, without knowing why, can find in the modern *palais de danse* something like a reconstruction of the perfect conditions of life within the mother's body. SUNDAY PICTORIAL

FOLIES PARISIENNE
SEE! NUDES IN THE WATERFALL
DARING FAN DANCE,
VIRGIN AND THE DEVIL
Sensational Dance of the Strip Apache
Les Beaux Mannequins de Parisienne
Continental and Oriental Nudes
Old Age Pensioners Monday
Advertisement in the ASHBY TIMES

☐ 'One can well understand those people who believe that intercourse is wrong except where children are concerned,' the judge said. 'That is a widely held and respectable view.'

He added that the husband believed that intimacy was repellent, unpleasant and something to be endured in order to have children. NEWS OF THE WORLD

☐ I went into a shop intending to buy some cheese. Seeing some flies hovering around the uncovered cheese I spoke to the assistant and was surprised to be told, 'They are fresh flies. They were not there yesterday.' *Letter in the* STAR

☐ A Norwich man and his wife on holiday at Southend went on a coach 'mystery' trip. The coach took them to – Norwich. They spent the day in the cattle market to avoid meeting friends. DAILY EXPRESS

☐ In the old days the adultress was stoned, but nowadays immorality seems to be quite accepted.
By all means look after the unfortunate babies, but a little bit of stoning might improve things all round. *Letter in the* GLASGOW BULLETIN

☐ As a small child out with my father I was watching a Guardsman on duty. As he passed us I said, in childish innocence, 'You've got a muff on your head.' My father reacted angrily. I got a good whack and he said, 'That is the Queen's uniform. Don't you ever dare say such a thing again.'
I never did. *Letter in the* NEWS CHRONICLE

☐ Reading on your page every week about what happens to many girls has made me realize there are not as many nice boys as I thought. *Letter in* WOMAN

☐ A split meeting of the Y.F.C. was held on Monday night, when the boys learned a great deal from a talk on artificial insemination by a representative from Southbar Cattle Breeding

Centre. The girls learned much about the arrangement of flowers from Miss Moira Grant, Busby, who demonstrated the art. After tea, the boys continued with their talk while the girls examined the floral arrangements more closely. HAMILTON ADVERTISER

□ 'It's not nice to be called a vice-chairman,' Councillor H. Eden told the Billinge Urban Council last night. So the council decided to discuss whether vice-chairman should become deputy chairman. GUARDIAN

□ Plymouth City Council yesterday took away its £100 grants from two Church homes for unmarried mothers and teenage girls and gave them instead to Plymouth Dogs and Cats Home. NEWS CHRONICLE

□ Speaking about a 16-year-old boy who was accused of offences against two girls, Mr Stephen Coates, a psychologist, said at Luton Juvenile Court: 'Previously he has been found guilty of offences which suggested a homosexual nature. These latest offences are at least evidence of a step in the right direction.' NEWS OF THE WORLD

□ Mrs Patricia Miller, of Kingston Hill, the club's rally organizer, said today: 'The object of the hunt is to give the members an idea of what actually happens. Those in at the kill will be 'blooded' with a mixture of tomato sauce and mud.' EVENING STANDARD

□ Because we believe there is something special in the relationship between us, we have always taken you into our confidence about important things. And now we have to tell you that, owing to the immense rise in the cost of production, we have been compelled to raise the price of our little magazine by one half-penny. WOMAN'S WEEKLY

□ I wondered why my bus was going so fast late at night. Then the conductor said: 'We're nipping along sharpish to miss the cinema crowd.' DAILY MIRROR

□ A dapper, white-bearded Cambridge professor told yesterday how he went to the local authority for sex education pamphlets for his two sons.
'But I was so alarmed in case my wife should see them I had to throw them out.' NEWS CHRONICLE

□ I knew a woman who named her son Gabriel, but she always called him Sidney. It was not until he left school that he discovered his real name. He was so embarrassed by it that he refused to show his birth certificate to anyone, refused to work and drifted into a life of crime. *Letter in the* DAILY HERALD

□ I am engaged to a wonderful man, but lately he has become very moody and is always hitting me. He says it is nothing to what I shall get after marriage, and I must get used to being 'kept under control'. Please advise me: I want to marry him, but don't know how to handle the situation. *Letter in* WOMAN'S OWN

□ A man who 'rather fancied' a young woman cashier in a Birmingham bank wrote a number of notes to her at the bank, turned up disguised as a blind beggar and serenaded her on a piano-accordion, and finally arrived at the bank dressed in tennis clothes and turned somersaults in front of the staff. MANCHESTER GUARDIAN

□ We are having a couple to dinner next week who are very well connected and I am a little nervous. Is it correct to watch the telly both before and after dinner? *Letter in the* EVENING STANDARD

□ People living on the new N.C.B. estate in the village are unable to obtain a reasonable picture on their TV sets because there is not enough electric power in the village, the council was told.

'I have to go to bed at eight recently because I couldn't get a picture of any kind on my set,' complained Mr Peter McDonald. YORKSHIRE EVENING POST

□ I fell in love with my husband simply because he was so different from every other boy I had ever met. He did not like love-making and neither did I. He has never actually told me he loves me.

Now, after 26 years of marriage, I sometimes wonder if I have missed something, but I am happy. He is a wonderful husband.

He never actually proposed, but we saw a three-piece suite we liked and that clinched the idea. *Letter in the* DAILY HERALD

□ How can I get my two-year-old daughter interested in television? We sit her in front of the set. She watches for a minute and says: 'Switch it off, Mummy.' I should hate to think my daughter will grow up uninterested in TV. *Letter in the* DAILY MIRROR

□ Yesterday somebody who should know about it told me the ancient Greeks were homosexuals. If so, they were a thoroughly bad lot. It's high time we banned Greek from our schools and universities. NEWS CHRONICLE

□ Is any other reader afraid of the dustmen? When they call I always hide, just in case they say anything about the type of rubbish I put in the bin. *Letter in* REYNOLDS NEWS

□ A St Albans motorist, summoned at St Albans Divisional Sessions on Saturday for a driving offence, was asked by a police Inspector: 'After the accident, why did you raise your bowler hat to acknowledge the driver of the other car involved, when you did not know him?'

The motorist replied: 'The accident had caused the hat to become crammed down over my eyes and ears and – although it might have been polite to raise it to the other driver – I lifted it to alleviate my discomfort!' HERTS ADVERTISER

□ Police Constable Harry Powell, posing as a variety artist to get inside the Spare Wheel Club, Manchester, sang 'Good-bye' for club members, it was stated yesterday, when the club was struck off for serving drinks after hours. The prosecution said one man had to be restrained when Constable Powell sang. DAILY EXPRESS

□ Sex used to be treated with decent reticence – now it is discussed openly. This sort of thing can do immense harm. The moral standards accepted as 'normal' by most young people today are a case in point. Why our all-wise Creator should have chosen such a distasteful – even disgusting – means of reproducing humanity is a thing that I, personally, have never been able to understand. *Letter in the* BRISTOL EVENING POST

□ Have I joined the middle classes? I find myself calling my doctor and my solicitor by their Christian names – and that I'm told is a criterion of middle-class establishment. *Letter in the* SUNDAY GRAPHIC

□ George Featherstone walks three miles to work because a robin is nesting under the saddle of his motor-cycle. DAILY TELEGRAPH

□ Sir,

The thirtieth annual Foire Gastronomique, perhaps the greatest food fair in Europe, has just ended here at Dijon. The British stand (a poor thing, but our own) was displaying among other national delicacies, tins of cat and dog food. *Letter in* THE TIMES

□ As soon as you know an H-bomb is on the way, run out and paint your windows with a mixture of whitewash and curdled milk to deflect dangerous rays. Soak your curtains and upholstery with a solution of borax and starch to prevent fire. *Lecturer in civil defence reported in* REYNOLDS NEWS

□ The mother complained that her son, an only child, was becoming truculent, had started smoking, had been seen entering a public-house, and was keeping company with a girl.

Insp. McCann began to investigate. 'I found that the son was 36,' he states. BIRMINGHAM POST

□ Sir,

I do not think you are quite fair to British Railways or their employees. At 12 o'clock one recent Friday night I saw some happy railway porters folk-dancing on No. 2 platform at Basingstoke.

One would not have seen this before nationalization. *Letter in the* DAILY TELEGRAPH

□ I've been going steady with my boyfriend for two years and we both intend getting engaged – we're both 19. He says he'll never marry a girl who's not a virgin and so to be sure that I am one he wants to have intercourse with me before we become engaged. *Letter in* WOMANS OWN

□ The Post Office has apologized for reprimanding a Post Office fitter for giving a girl friend a lift in his van. The 'girl friend' was later established as being the fitter's apprentice mate, who has shoulder-length blonde hair. DAILY TELEGRAPH

□ Mrs Dimmock deplored the fact that young people no longer went into private service. She thought that, apart from the pleasant relationship that existed between employer and employee, the servant picked up a far better accent. WORTHING GAZETTE

□ Stepping over a pile of cats playing on the floor of her sitting-room, 52-year-old Mrs Payne said: 'Cyril needs mothering, but we are better friends apart. The trouble is that he prefers animals to humans. That has been the trouble all along. I do not think I would have minded so much if he collected other women the way most men do.' SUNDAY EXPRESS

□ A death with honour decision was made by the North-west Sussex Water Board at Horsham yesterday. A directive to the board's bailiffs allows them to shoot cormorants suspected of eating any of the £1,700 worth of trout which are to restock Crawley's Wear Wood reservoir at Forest Row. But 'to be fair' to the dead birds a post-mortem examination will be made to establish their guilt or innocence. GUARDIAN

□ Indians who use Nuneaton public slipper baths are using so much hot water that Nuneaton Borough Council proposes to charge them a special rate. A Council official said today: 'These Indians do not bath like English people. They first scrub themselves in a bath of hot water and the process is repeated with a second bathful. Then they have it filled a third time to rinse their bodies.

All this is running away with the hot water supply. We are going to explain the position to the Indians and will have to charge them for each bathful.'
BIRMINGHAM MAIL

☐ Mr Mervyn Griffith-Jones, prosecuting counsel, opposing the application, said: 'It is a perfectly ordinary little case of a man charged with indecency with four or five guardsmen.' GUARDIAN

☐ The Dartmoor prison debating society last week passed a resolution expressing the hope that the Conservative Party would be returned at the next General Election. Other resolutions by the prisoners asked for a reintroduction of corporal punishment and hanging.
OBSERVER

☐ Am I unreasonable? I have been married for 12 years and have a family, and my husband recently asked me to be intimate with him on the back seat of our car. This happened in the heart of the country and I agreed. I am now worried because I am sure this is very wrong. Please help me. *Letter in the* DAILY MIRROR

☐ The four-letter words in *Lady Chatterley* are not likely to be included in the Oxford Dictionary as a result of the case. 'This legal judgment is irrelevant to our purpose,' said Oxford University Press. 'We don't take into account anything but common usage.'
DAILY EXPRESS

☐ 'We choose a number of men from the studio audience,' said Mr Philip Wedge, AR's Manager of Quiz Programmes. 'We tie ladies' corsets round their waists, and the first to get their corsets off and hold them above their heads are put on the programme. We find this gives us the right sort of contestant in a high proportion of cases.'
EVENING STANDARD

☐ I wonder how much the biology lectures to children in school lead to sex experiments in teenagers of today. In my youth we were taught that babies came as a result of prayer. *Letter in the* WEST LONDON PRESS

☐ Scotland Yard is searching for more space in which to store its embarrassingly large stock of obscene books and pictures, and HM Customs is forbidden to burn any more obscene books because they were breaking the rules of a smokeless zone by making black smoke.
GUARDIAN

☐ 'My ambition is to walk out of Wimbledon Town Hall and have all the kids rip my clothes off for souvenirs – because it'll show I've arrived.' *Pop singer reported in the* DAILY EXPRESS

☐ Interested as I am in our survival as a nation, I would give all the works of Shakespeare, Chaucer, Milton, Keats, Shelley, the lot, for just one armoured brigade. *Columnist in the* EVENING NEWS

☐ A man walked into the police station at Royston, Hertfordshire, and told Police Constable Victor Cripps that he had something to surrender under the firearms amnesty. He then handed over a small anti-tank gun, four service rifles, 12,000 rounds of ammunition, several live hand grenades and three German booby traps, described as 'fairly dangerous'. GUARDIAN

☐ A grey-haired widow wept when told she could not put a photograph of her husband on his grave. The decision was made by Hornchurch Council, Essex, which said: 'We can't allow it. We must have uniformity among the graves.' DAILY EXPRESS

□ During the last six months I have knocked over no fewer than four cyclists. On each occasion the cyclist was entirely to blame. In future I shall let them take the consequences of their own folly, and make no effort to avoid them. *Letter in the* SUN

□ My husband is a shy man and whenever he brings flowers home to me he always conceals them under his bowler hat. As a result they have to be little flowers like violets or anemones and tend to smell of brilliantine. Surely there must be some other way in which self-conscious men cope with this problem? *Letter in* TODAY

□ My husband does not GIVE me my housekeeping allowance – he HIDES it. He puts pound notes in odd places all over the sitting-room, and makes me look for them. I can never be quite sure how many to expect, and I am scared stiff that I will miss one or two. *Letter in the* DAILY HERALD

□ Not more than two 'deaths' a year will be permitted in the 'Emergency Ward 10' series on Independent Television. The script writers were told of this policy yesterday. Previously as many as four or five 'deaths' a year occurred in the series. On each occasion the public reacted unfavourably. Incurable diseases have been banned from the programme. DAILY TELEGRAPH

□ When my twins were small, I very often occupied their play-pen when doing needlework and mending. In this way I obtained isolated peace, and the twins had more space in the room to use up their energies. *Letter in the* SUNDAY EXPRESS

□ For murderings of policemen, prison officers, security men, and for murderings for robbery, I would suggest amputations of both legs up to the body, plus prison for 10 years, with no artificial limbs ever in the offing. Only a small cart on very small wheels. That would be the main deterrent. Further violence, if any, could be dealt with by further deformities. *Letter in the* HUDDERSFIELD DAILY EXAMINER

□ At 11.59 p.m. on 14 November, about 300 people will set off on a five-mile hike to the 762ft summit of Ivinghoe Beacon, in Hertfordshire. They will carry with them aspidistras in pots, or objects and plants resembling aspidistras, to take part in the World Aspidistra Show. At the summit, they will compete in a so-called nut-cracking contest which entails pushing a block of wood round a marked course with their heads in the pitch dark. EVENING STANDARD

□ I do not like wasting time when I watch TV on my own. I like to do something else at the same time. I do foot, finger and eye exercises. I shrug my shoulders and roll my head round and round. During the Wimbledon tournament, whenever the players changed ends I went down on my back to do a few tummy exercises and circled my legs round in the air. *Letter in the* DAILY HERALD

□ A fisherman, Miles Johnson, of Bank Hook, Southport, said at an inquest there yesterday that he had seen a man walking fully clothed into the sea, but did not speak to him because 'in the past when I have warned people about danger, I've been told to mind my own business'. GUARDIAN

□ South Coast Electric Carriage Society invited applications from first-class conversational gentlemen to fill vacancy

113

among old-established commuters. Club premises, 8 a.m. Worthing–Hove–Victoria. *Advertisement in* THE TIMES

☐ Undertaker George Frederick Marsland, of Old Street, Ashton, told Ashton magistrates today that his 'busy' season is approaching. He was applying successfully for the lifting of a driving ban imposed in February for being in charge of a van while under the influence of drink. MANCHESTER EVENING NEWS

☐ Bringing up the rear of the parade will be a float contributed by the Institute of Directors. It will show 'the workers of Great Britain making an all-out effort to get our exports to the world's markets'. GUARDIAN

☐ While endorsing your correspondent Mr H. Gray's view that Liberals should be allotted as much broadcasting time as Conservatives and Socialists, I must protest at his derogatory reference to 'flat earthers'. The International Flat Earth Society is a thriving scientific body, and it would be a pity for it to be derided by those who have not really studied the subject. *Letter in the* GUARDIAN

☐ I was most intrigued by your note on the glass-blower's 'Frigging' in last October's issue. This surely must be the origin of the expression 'frigging about' meaning doodling or wasting one's time. I thought it an expression peculiar to Pembrokeshire, but recently I heard a Yorkshireman from Hull use it and I have never heard that Pembs. had any special connexion with the glass-making industry. *Letter in* TOWN AND COUNTRY

☐ We went to France for our holidays and took six large sliced loaves of bread with us. We still had one left after 13 days. It was still good to eat. This is a tribute to a Leicester bakery. *Letter in the* LEICESTER MERCURY

☐ Last night a Co-operative Stores official said: 'We have another Father Christmas now. We are sorry about Mr Bates because he was so popular with the children. But we couldn't have him giving away toys.' DAILY MAIL

☐ Everybody should know how to perform 'kiss-of-life' respiration, but it is undesirable that the method should be practised freely for training purposes, says Surgeon Captain Stanley Miles, R.N., in *Family Journal*, the British Medical Association magazine. THE TIMES

☐ I must say we really enjoy all the commercials in our household, but I always get a tense feeling in case anyone picks the wrong pile of washing in that detergent advertisement. *Letter in* TV TIMES

☐ My weekly treat is a visit to a small local cinema. The manager there knows almost every customer. I have a seat booked at the end of the back row, and as I suffer from bad feet the manager allows me the luxury of bathing my feet in hot water during the show. I fill up the bowl in his office. You do not get service like this in the big posh cinemas. *Letter in* REVEILLE

☐ When my husband is away I cannot bear to watch a BBC thriller because there are no breaks to return me to reality. I enjoy ITV thrillers because the advertisement breaks – clothes going round in a washing machine, and fresh young teenagers popping sweets into their mouths – allow me to shake off the horror and return for another session. *Letter in the* DAILY HERALD

☐ How do you get into the minds of young people these days? I'll tell you how I succeeded. My daughter had broken a plant pot in her room a week ago and yesterday the pieces were still lying on the floor.

I had had enough. I borrowed a toy revolver from my son, and donned a mask. As she came in, with a tense command, 'Git goin'' I forced her at gunpoint up to her room and indicated the job to be done. Instead of snarling, 'Ya can't git away with this,' she cleared up the mess and brightly inquired, 'What's for tea, mummy?' *Letter in the* DAILY EXPRESS

☐ 'Do you gents want something to drink?' though said in a perfectly friendly manner, was not, in my view, the right way for a wine waiter to address First Class passengers. SUNDAY TIMES

☐ There were four of us in the doctor's waiting room when in walked a Pakistani. He was about to go straight into the surgery when a woman jumped up and grabbed his arm, saying in very deliberate English: 'We are before you. You take your turn. Understand?' The Pakistani, in equally deliberate English, replied: 'No, you are after me. Me doctor. Understand?' DAILY MIRROR

☐ He never washed up anything, so the kitchen was awful. He used every plate, every piece of cutlery in the house, and these just remained stacked up by the sink, week after week. To me, this way of life was distinctly bohemian and exciting. It was the right background for our first experiments in sex. *Mary Quant in the* SUNDAY MIRROR

☐ The sexual habits of the Pakistanis arouse a variety of interesting comments, some of which reveal as much about local mores as about the immigrants. One young woman I met in Bradford said they had all kinds of perverted

customs: they even made the women take off all their clothes before sexual intercourse. OBSERVER

☐When I glimpse the backs of women's knees I seem to hear the first movement of Beethoven's Pastoral Symphony. *Charles Greville,* DAILY MAIL

☐ It was difficult to get into Saudi Arabia and unthinkable for a woman to travel alone. She had great difficulty in obtaining a visa, but once there Mrs Iggulden had a marvellous time. Mrs Iggulden witnessed the public floggings and mutilations of Yemeni saboteurs. She was invited to have coffee in the desert with a bedouin tribesman, and found them a kind, gentle people who would do anything for the visitor, she said. HERNE BAY PRESS

☐ (Said) John Crittle of Dandie Fashions in the King's road: 'Underpants? No, we don't sell them, There's no money in them. Anyway, men don't buy their briefs in men's shops, they go up the road to the girls' shop.' Mr Crittle revealed, under questioning, that he was currently wearing a pair of ladies' red briefs trimmed with lace. SUNDAY MIRROR

☐ What nonsense to suggest, as your women's page did last week, that the use of a dummy is either unhygienic or a bad habit which could become hard for baby to break. I have derived great comfort from my dummy for over 40 years, and find it gives much greater oral satisfaction than the unhealthy cigarette. It is also much cheaper. *Letter in the* BRIGHTON AND HOVE HERALD

☐ Unlike Mr Eric Mallett, I have written the truth in a boarding home visitor's book (Dear Sir: 21 August). Asked for my comments I wrote: 'A grand holiday ruined by poor food and disgusting accommodation.' Monday morning brought a letter demanding a written apology by return post or, failing this, legal action would be taken. *Letter in* TIT-BITS

☐ The annual contest between the universities of Oxford and Cambridge kicked off at 12 noon yesterday in the East car park at Twickenham. The strangest Bacchanalia of middle-class Britain got going some two hours before the game's kick-off when a man using an empty champagne bottle as a bat belted a cork at a policeman at square leg. The policeman, knowing he was dealing with the middle classes, smiled. DAILY MAIL

☐ UNCERTAIN (*Tea at Bachelor's Flat*). So far as your first inquiry is concerned, the host will choose whether or not he asks his guest to pour out. He will probably do so, but she should not offer. It is socially proper to add the milk after the tea, but many people do it the other way round, because they prefer the quite certainly different taste. I think that, in this case, the best thing to do is simply to say 'Milk first or last?' thus showing that you know the 'correct' thing to do. LADY

☐ Waitresses used eyebrow tweezers to remove flakes of rust in dishes of jelly at Bath's Pump Room. And Councillor Will Johns, who told this story to the city council last night, asked that in future the eyebrow tweezers be sterilized. WESTERN DAILY PRESS

☐ Councillor Harry Wells told Windsor Council's general purposes committee meeting: 'I was shocked at the lack of morals. There were young girls having their navels and breasts painted with flowers in broad daylight. At night couples were carrying on acts of immorality. I was in the Guards and I know what they were up to!' DAILY SKETCH

☐ Cemetery superintendent Frank Maule is delighted with his farewell present from his employers. He has been given a grave space. DAILY MAIL

☐ Empty two cans of condensed cream of asparagus soup into a saucepan and add required amount of extra liquid. Stir to blend well and then heat gently until just under boiling point. If liked, add one large can cut asparagus spears, drained from tin. Reheat, but do not boil, and serve. *Recipe in the* TIMES SATURDAY REVIEW

☐ If an actor starts meditating on such problems as historical, philosophical or social questions, then he has doubts – this way he can say goodbye to the big money. I read books like mad, but I'm very careful not to let anything I read influence me. Otherwise, it's goodbye money and all the things that go with it. Goodbye electricity, gas, beautiful women. *Michael Caine in* WOMANS OWN

☐ Mathematical rules have now been devised to allow pedestrians to remain as dry as possible when caught in a shower of rain. The calculations were reported in *Nature* yesterday by Mr M. Scott, a mathematician at Durham University. When walking into the rain one should lower the head and walk as fast as possible. When the rain is coming from behind one should either walk forward leaning backwards or backward leaning forwards, at a deliberate pace. SUNDAY TELEGRAPH

☐ I went into a big store in town and asked the assistant for a small packet of **washing** powder. She handed me a packet marked 'Large'. 'I'm afraid you didn't understand,' I said. 'I asked for a small packet.' 'That's right, madam,' said the assistant. 'It comes in three sizes – Large, Giant and Super. I gave you the small size – Large.' *Letter in the* COMPETITOR'S JOURNAL

☐ Make the finishing touch the Besca toilet seat, of Polyester foam bonded on to chipboard. Covered in vinyl with an 'antique leather' surface, it is scrubbable in black, white, blue, green, turquoise, primrose or pink at 72s. 6d. Stuart or Black Watch tartans, bronze, and floral patterns are 77s. 6d. So is a Back-Britain model with a white seat and a Union Jack lid. FINANCIAL TIMES

☐ The boot isn't very big but a man from the factory warned me about that. He told me: 'A Rolls-Royce owner's luggage, sir, should precede him by rail or air.' AA MOTORIST'S MAGAZINE

☐ My bridegroom's first words to me when I joined him at the altar were, 'Who are you?' It made me think that the hours I spent on myself before going to church were all worth while. *Letter in the* DAILY MIRROR

☐ Referring to the story headed 'Emigrating With His Family' which appeared in last week's *Herald*, we wish to point out that Mr Terence Smith, whose future position in Australia was described as that of 'ordinary representative' will in fact be working as an assurance consultant. As his work is of a professional nature, the word 'colleague' is a more accurate description of Mr Smith's friend than 'workmate' as stated in the opening paragraph. CROSBY HERALD

☐ Colonel G. F. Perkins has retired from the board of Southern Newspapers Ltd after 30 years' service as a director, in order to make way for a younger man. Colonel Perkins's son, Major Christopher E. S. Perkins, has been elected as a director. ADVERTISER'S WEEKLY

☐ Mr Curry, who is the Maidstone agent, said: 'They were planning to call the get-together a cheese and wine party until I pointed out to them that it was illegal. We didn't want to get into trouble so we changed the name. We thought if we called it "cheese and you know what" everyone would think of wine. It's rather unfortunate.' DAILY MIRROR

☐ There are few *Vogue* readers who have never harboured a slinking desire to be thrown across the saddle of a plunging white stallion, galloped to a palmy oasis and stuffed with dates in a striped silk prison by swarthy warriors. VOGUE

☐ 'It was not racial feeling that made them smash the window,' he added, 'As they themselves will tell you, they did it as a normal part of hooliganism which occurs in any town.' LEAMINGTON SPA COURIER

☐ When my husband reads in bed on warm nights he puts a collander over his head. He says it keeps off the flies, shades his eyes from the light and lets in air at the same time. *Letters in* GOOD SHOPPING

☐ 'I have found that if you don't lock the bathroom some people are taking baths every day.' *Mr J. Glenton, member of Morecambe Hotels and Caterers Association, during a discussion on bathing habits of holiday visitors.* MORECAMBE GUARDIAN

Governmental control

☐ There were floral displays by the parks committees of Salford, Bolton, St Helens, Stretford, Urmston, Cheadle and Gatley, Ashton-under-Lyne, Stalybridge and Manchester.

'We awarded first prizes to all of them,' said the secretary and show manager Mr R. C. McMillan. 'We didn't want any jealousy among the ratepayers.' NEWS CHRONICLE

☐ Members were faced with the problem of what colour a lavatory wall should be. Mrs Davies wanted the walls of the Shawfields recreation ground one to be grey-green. Then Mr A. F. Steel declared that many people were superstitious and he said, quite seriously, they would not use the place if the walls were green. ALDERSHOT NEWS AND MILITARY GAZETTE

☐ An appeal against Esher Council's refusal to allow an illuminated sign at Hurst Service Station, East Moseley, has been allowed by the Minister of Housing and Local Government subject to certain conditions. One is that the sign shall not be illuminated. ESHER NEWS

☐ The smell of fish and chips floats over Richmond's quiet old-world Yorkshire market place from nearby shops six days a week.

Now the town's improvements committee wants the smell on Sundays too. They think it will attract visitors. NEWS CHRONICLE

☐ Showing of *Snow White and the Seven Dwarfs* will be given at a Durham Cinema tomorrow for the city magistrates to decide whether the film is fit for children unaccompanied by adults. NEWS CHRONICLE

☐ The Parish council at Woodville, Derbyshire, have ordered a street lamp to be moved because it sheds more light in the neighbouring district of Swadlincote than it does in Woodville. NEWS CHRONICLE

□ The campaign against the grey squirrel – now declared Public Pest No. 1 by the Forestry Commission, which has offered 1s. a tail – has been suspended because the squirrels are mating. Young squirrels might be left to starve in their nests. HAMPSTEAD AND HIGHGATE EXPRESS

□ The staff may not accept gratuities and may not sell or fetch sweets or refreshments for visitors, or receive letters at the conveniences. *Notice in Charlton Park*

□ A motor horse-box carrying a live horse can travel at 30 m.p.h. If the horse dies in transit the vehicle immediately becomes a carrier of horse-flesh and by law must reduce speed to 20 m.p.h. DAILY MAIL

□ Pauline Gough is only eight, but local officialdom decreed yesterday that every day she will have to walk 5½ miles along lonely lanes to and from school. Her seven-year-old sister Sheila will make the same journey alone in a six-seater taxi. The taxi will call for the younger sister, but must refuse the vacant seats to the girl one year older. NEWS CHRONICLE

□ New regulations announced yesterday for London's St James's and Green Parks remove the ban on pushing bathchairs more than three abreast. DAILY EXPRESS

□ Middlesex County Council is to be represented in Twickenham Fair procession by the West Middlesex main drainage department.

It is exhibiting a tableau of three decorated vehicles the stages through which sewage passes. SURREY COMET

□ Embarrassed Berkshire County Council officials have had to scrap hundreds of question forms sent out to expectant mothers who apply for polio injections.

Reason: In addition to their names, ages and addresses, the mothers-to-be were asked to fill in their sex. REYNOLDS NEWS

□ The danger of the Queen Mother's high-heeled shoes catching in the tram-lines outside Sheffield town hall posed a problem for corporation engineers yesterday.

But they soon hit on the solution. They diverted the city's trams for two hours and laid tarmac across the lines. SUNDAY DISPATCH

□ A woman, aged 90, who eighteen months ago was committed to a hospital for the aged against her will, was summoned at Chesterfield yesterday for failing to pay £482 15s. 6d., the cost of keeping her in hospital. GUARDIAN

□ The automatic flushing system of a 'gents' at Totnes (Devon) Guildhall will be stopped when the Queen visits the town on 27 July – so that the noise does not disturb the Royal party. It has also been suggested that guests should stand in a semi-circle – to hide the entrance. SUNDAY PICTORIAL

□ A health committee's report to the council recommends that unmarried expectant mothers, age 16 or under, may stay at home from school longer than the usual 12 weeks. DAILY MAIL

☐ Farmers at West Hythe were this week asked to move their cattle away from an area being used during an Army demonstration week – because the cows have a habit of standing and staring at visiting parties of high-ranking officers watching demonstrations. KENTISH EXPRESS

☐ Two rabbits – one of each sex – may be kept as pets by council house tenants in Ripley, Derbyshire, so that their children can 'learn something about the birds and the bees'. DAILY MAIL

☐ Council officials and landladies agreed at South Shields yesterday that a 25 per cent increase in local holiday inquiries $3\frac{1}{2}$ months before the start of the season was due mostly to the publicity the town received by its typhoid outbreak last summer. DAILY TELEGRAPH

☐ Council workmen are to rip planks out of seats and make holes in the walls of bus shelters – in an attempt to make the shelters too uncomfortable for hooligans. ... Councillor Harry Bill said: 'Something has got to be done to stop the wrecking of these shelters. So far as I can see this is the only way.' SUN

☐ Some long-service railwaymen, on retirement, are invited to public presentations, praised for their loyalty, and given a cheque for £5. Afterwards British Railways deduct the money from the men's pensions. GUARDIAN

☐ At Grantham, Lincs, tarmac will be laid 120 yards down an unmade road to give the Queen Mother a smooth drive when she opens an old folks' home on Wednesday. Afterwards the £300 surface will be ripped up. SUNDAY MIRROR

☐ The man from the Ministry in Edinburgh confessed yesterday that it was a 'gritty problem'. He added, 'We have not been able to make great progress. I can tell you, though, that we are at the moment stirring it up a bit. We are taking stock of the situation, but since we haven't yet taken stock, I cannot say, of course, what we have taken stock of.' It was, he said, 'an urgent thing that we should want to see done, but on the longer-term basis of urgently.' SCOTSMAN

☐ A maze to muddle motorists is the basis of a plan drawn up by Westminster City Council to create in Pimlico an environmental area with traffic kept to a minimum. It is hoped that through-motorists will be so perplexed they will not enter the area again. DAILY TELEGRAPH

☐ Model-maker Mr Sidney Hayes has been told that figures of the Beatles, Black and White Minstrels, Andy Pandy and other personalities must be moved out of his front garden. The half-size models, say Bridge-Blean rural council, near Canterbury, Kent, were put in the garden without planning permission. SUN

☐ At all events, Breconshire seems the one place where maternity beds ought not to be at a premium in March. Elsewhere the situation is different. 'I'm sorry, sir,' a colleague was told by the almoner of one Midland maternity hospital in September, 'but if your wife needs a bed in March it should have been booked 10 months in advance.' THE TIMES

☐ 'We welcome sleepers here,' the Librarian of Cambridge University said yesterday. 'A sleeping reader is less of a menace to the books than a waking one.' THE TIMES

The law courts

□ A submission that a pedestrian could not possibly be a vehicle was upheld by Willesden Magistrates yesterday. BIRMINGHAM POST

□ Police Constable Roy Rushmore, booked by a fellow policeman for parking, told Ipswich magistrates yesterday: 'I had to attend this court as a witness. I knew that 20 minutes is the parking limit except with special permission from a uniformed policeman. I was in uniform and there was no other policeman about so I gave myself permission.' NEWS CHRONICLE

□ A young painter who drove a borrowed car over a canvas spread out in a Kensington mews to produce an 'action' picture, was fined 10s at West London yesterday for driving without a licence. DAILY TELEGRAPH

□ She continued to dance around the floor allowing the folds to fall to two thicknesses, through which the upper part of her body could be seen plainly. Then she advanced to within two feet of some of the customers, withdrawing and replacing the veil, added the officer. Said Chief Supt. Arthur Drury, prosecuting: 'I appreciate your limitations but can you show their worships how she did it?' And P.C. Kirsop picked up the green-backed oath card from the witness-box, held it over his chest and lowered and raised it quickly to show the pockets of his uniform tunic. NEWS OF THE WORLD

□ Mr W. Rees, the Chief Constable of Stockport, has reminded members of his Force that when cycling they should propel the pedals with the ball of the foot and not the instep. From the point of view of public appearance, he stated, he hoped the practice of pedalling with the instep, and leaving the front of the foot protruding, would cease. POLICE REVIEW

□ There were murmurs of disapproval from a defence solicitor. Mr Peter Smith, prosecuting for Havering Council, rose to inform puzzled magistrates: 'I think my friend is disturbed because the witness has taken the oath on a steak and kidney pie.' HORNCHURCH ECHO

□ Mr Jeremy Gompertz (for both men) told the assistant chairman that they had not intended using the ammonia against a human being. They thought they might run into a guard dog in the museum. Judge Block said: 'I think the idea of using it on a dog is rather worse than using it on a human being.' BRIGHTON ARGUS

The churches

□ It was surely for such a purpose as the Coronation service that God created television. *Letter in* PICTURE POST

□ In view of the appalling harvest I should like to suggest that the normal Harvest Festival services are either suspended altogether or modified in some way to register our disappointment. *Letter in the* LEICESTER MERCURY

□ Asked to comment on the new campaign, an official of the Lord's Day Observance Society said last night: 'We don't give statements on Sundays.' NEWS CHRONICLE

□ Father Alfred Baldwin, the priest in charge of St Anne's Church, Buxton, has bought an acre of lunar land from the Inter-Planetary Development Corporation in New York as a site for the first church on the moon. MANCHESTER GUARDIAN

□ The Archbishop of Canterbury, Dr Fisher, said at a Nairobi banquet today that the divorce rate in Britain is 'as beastly as Mau Mau'. DAILY EXPRESS

□ A bishop's idea of reducing road deaths on a dangerous stretch of the Great North Road brought protests yesterday. The Bishop of Grantham, the Right Rev. A. Otter, suggested 'a few skeletons dangling over the road' along a stretch, south of Grantham, where in the past twelve months thirteen people have been killed. A Methodist minister, the Rev. A. J. Bowers, said yesterday that the bishop's suggestion was 'sadistically crude' and a resident called it 'barbaric'. GUARDIAN

☐ The wartime leader of the 51st, Major-General D. M. Wimberley, Coupar-Angus, said about religion: 'When I was with the division in battle, I said my prayers at night and then handed the division over to God for his keeping. Then when I woke in the morning I took it back again.' GLASGOW HERALD

☐ Since it has been definitely proved that the smoking habit is injurious to health, would it not be helpful to direct research to discover the purpose for which the tobacco plant was made? ('And God saw everything that He had made, and, behold, it was very good.') The tobacco companies will then be given the opportunity to reverse their present unhappy position by producing something which will be of lasting benefit to the race, and of greater profit to themselves. *Letter in the* EDINBURGH EVENING NEWS

☐ Hanging, a clergyman suggested yesterday, might be 'theologically and intellectually, rather a good way to die'. DAILY MIRROR

☐ 'I don't believe there is total sexual satisfaction outside Jesus Christ,' exclaimed Dr Graham. Dr Graham will adopt a neutral attitude to the problems of Vietnam and Rhodesia. EVENING STANDARD

☐ I have a pet budgerigar, which has a swing in its cage. I have made a practice of disconnecting this swing each Sunday and not putting it back into use until Monday morning. Is this in accord with strict Christian principle? *Letter in the* BELFAST NEWS LETTER

☐ 'Fortunately we're insured against Acts of God,' said the vicar after lightning struck, sending rafters crashing down on the church altar. ACTON GAZETTE

☐ I cannot help wondering why God created coloured people, seeing all the resultant difficulties caused thereby. CHURCH TIMES

☐ Our first parents – Adam and Eve – were white. How then did the coloured races come into existence? This intriguing question baffles me. *Letter in the* DAILY MAIL

☐ Cast-off altar cloths make excellent curtains. A Westminster Cathedral spokesman for the Roman Catholic Church in England told me: 'There is nothing against this from our point of view. Sacred furnishings which have worn out lose their blessing when they are sold on the open market.' SUN

The changing pattern of sport

☐ Fans at Glasgow White City speedway track are complaining that there isn't enough smell about the dirt track now that odourless fuel is used in the bikes.

The smell, apparently, creates atmosphere. So the management has arranged for an old car, filled with the crudest oil one can get, to run around the track before and after each race. DAILY MAIL

☐ Hunts like the North Warwickshire, which borders the M1, have found that foxes can nip across the motorways leaving the hunt either to call the hounds in or risk disastrous accidents with fast-moving vehicles. The Duke of Beaufort has a better idea. He has a scheme to erect a special chain-link fence along the section of the M4 crossing his country. This will prevent cattle, horsemen, hounds – and foxes – from straying across it. About 20 miles of fencing may be necessary at £1 a yard. Total cost: £35,000. DAILY EXPRESS

☐ I don't think it is at all polite the way bowlers rub the ball all over themselves at cricket. *Letter in the* MANCHESTER EVENING NEWS

☐ Every room in a £687,000 motel-cum-leisure centre to be built at Southport, Lancs, will be carpeted with artificial turf so golfing guests can practise putting in privacy. SUNDAY MIRROR

☐ Meads was kicked on the head, and had to have three stitches put in the cut. Kirkpatrick broke his nose early in the match. Villepreux played most of the game with two ribs broken. Many others were hurt. Some of the injuries were deliberately inflicted. These deeds made unpleasant watching. But, taken as a whole, this was not a game that got out of hand. GUARDIAN

The Englishman and his responsibilities to the earwig, the porpoise, the pigeon and the snail, to the kitten, the fox and the hedgehog, to the tit tribe and to horses, to worms and to caterpillars, dogs and fleas

☐ At a neighbour's suggestion I tied old sacking around the base of my apple tree to trap insects. The first time I moved it I found hundreds of earwigs. Just as I was about to destroy them I remembered reading that earwigs are devoted mothers, risking anything to protect their young. I replaced the sacking without killing one. Needless to say there isn't an apple fit to eat. *Letter in the* PEOPLE

☐ In last week's issue of the *Falmouth Packet* we published details of a Penryn resident's encounter with a porpoise climbing the steps at Penryn Quay. This was an incorrect report due to a bad telephone connexion. What the man really saw coming up the steps was a coypu, an animal which is similar in appearance to a large rat or an otter. We regret any inconvenience which we may have caused by our erroneous report. FALMOUTH PACKET

☐ Firemen climbed a 60 ft ladder to the roof of the Royal Exchange in London yesterday – to rescue a pigeon. Someone reported in a 999 call that it was being attacked by another pigeon. In fact it was being fed. DAILY MAIL

☐ A 7in. edible snail was caught at London Airport yesterday after it had hidden on a Comet from Nairobi and Benghazi. The snail was taken to the RSPCA hostel. DAILY MAIL

☐ One of the original kittens had been killed by the Mau Mau and his preserved body was flown to England, said Miss Cotton. She went on: 'He was the son of a cat whose picture appeared on National Savings posters. We felt it was only right for him to be buried in his own country.' DAILY MIRROR

☐ Fox-hunting Lady Anne Fitzalan-Howard, 21-year-old daughter of the Duke of Norfolk, has a date in the church hall near her father's castle on Friday with the local branch of the British Union for the Abolition of Vivisection. Wondering how Lady Anne reconciles her support for this cause with her own love of fox-hunting, I phoned her. Angrily she said: 'There is no connexion. One is sport and the other is downright cruelty.' SUNDAY DISPATCH

☐ A Portsmouth man believes he has found the way to talk to hedgehogs – although he does not know the meaning of what he says to them. EVENING NEWS

☐ Dr Maurice Burton, in his note about the habit of certain members of the tit tribe of drinking from milk bottles, is puzzled by the occasional appearance of little stones at the bottom of the bottles after these visitations. Could it be that these highly intelligent, and I am sure honourable small birds are paying for the milk? Letter in the DAILY TELEGRAPH

☐ 'There ought to be a regular births and deaths column for horses. It is a splendid idea and I hope it catches on. A regular column where people can keep up with the news of horses they once knew or rode is definitely needed.' Report in DAILY HERALD

☐ It is because of unnecessary cruelty to worms that I would also suggest the prohibition of all games on grass. I once saw a beautiful worm unnecessarily killed by a rugby player's boot, and no doubt death by violence must be caused to millions of these useful creatures by the pursuit of balls. Letter in the WESTERN MAIL

☐ As the 700 men taking part in the Freedom parade approached the saluting base, a woman in the crowd noticed a caterpillar making a desperate attempt to cross the road.

'Quick, rescue that caterpillar,' she cried, and her plea was heard by the man standing next to her, who dashed into the road and saved the tiny creature from certain death by popping it into his pocket. HUNTS POST

☐ Public conveniences for dogs should be set up in streets and squares, the National Canine Defence League urges. In its journal it suggests the name 'dog pennies'. . . . 'The idea of a convenience for dogs may sound amusing. Conveniences for human beings were an amusing idea only 50 years ago, and in some of our large cities at that.' NEWS CHRONICLE

☐ I find to my delight that I can make my dog happy by wagging its tail for it. Letter in REVEILLE

☐ Even in the flea circus times have changed. I talked to flea impresario Alfred Testo.

'We used to get fleas from cranedrivers' socks in a Hartlepools steel works,' he said. 'Now, with all these disinfectants about, we have to advertise for them in the papers.' EVENING STANDARD

☐ But, if he was a sage in business hours, he was always a boy at heart. The heart was given over to birds, beasts and flowers. He was an eager field naturalist and gardener, a still keener shot. And like most great English killers of birds he was a merciful man who cherished the victims he slew so cleanly. THE TIMES